DEDICATED TO

My oldest son "Bubba", who at the early age of 9 years old started on his career in the taxidermist business along with me. At first it was the minor things, such as sweeping the floors and keeping the table tops tidy. As time moved on however, he took on all aspects of the trade, and especially the painting of fish. Today he has attained the speed and skill in painting of one much older. His continued progress in the operations of the business has taken a lot of the burden off his old dad. Thanks again son for your years of help and dedication.

CONTENTS

INTRODUCTION

The purpose of this book is to teach the basic and advanced methods of fish mounting.

For years the mystery of fish mounting remained in the back rooms of old established taxidermy shops, and up to date material was not available to the beginning taxidermist.

After thirty years of trial and error and many disappointments later, we developed several good methods for mounting, and presented them in this book illustrated with numerous photographs and drawings in an easy to follow "step by step" format. In my years of experience I have learned that there are as many methods as there are taxidermists, and we have only attempted to show those that we think are easy to learn as well as those that have commercial applications.

The art of taxidermy takes time and patience to perfect no matter what it is that you are trying to mount, but it is enjoyable as well as challenging whether it is a hobby or a profession. This book is written for the professional and the beginner in that it should be easy enough for even the youngest taxidermist to follow and the professional who has mounted fish before should find many new and innovative ideas in this book. I have tried to include everything from the beginning stages of fish mounting to the final step of painting and leave nothing to question.

Some of the methods I will spend more time on because I think that they merit more attention than others. I will try to be as objective as possible and give the advantages and disadvantages of all the methods that are covered.

The need for a complete fish mounting book is quite evident when you consider that 27 million people will go fishing this year for bass alone. According to the national survey of the Department of the Interior, a total of 40 million people in the U.S. will go fishing. Everybody likes a trophy to remember their trips by, and the taxidermist will continue to service the needs of these people.

This book is for the person who wants to mount an occasional fish that he catches, as well as for others who will be starting on a career in professional taxidermy where they will eventually encounter every facet of taxidermy.

Fish mounting can be started on a shoestring and move into a fulltime occupation in a short time if the student is serious, and not afraid of the long hours and hard work involved in establishing a business. I don't know of any business that can be started with less capital and done at home, or in a small shop. Of course, how far you go in fish taxidermy will ultimately depend upon you. This book is a tool that must be used along with hard work and a determination to learn on your part.

There is a great deal of work in this country crying to be done, and in many sections of this country, there isn't a fish taxidermist within a 100 mile radius.

Most of the materials that I will mention can be purchased locally, or made according to our instructions. Many other items can be purchased from taxidermy supply houses.

Fish Skinning - (Largemouth Bass)

When you are ready to mount your first fish it will be to your advantage to choose the largemouth bass or a similar scaled fish as your first specimen because they are easiest to mount.

Because the largemouth bass is the most sought after mount in the United States, it will be our subject fish throughout the entire book. We also use this fish as an example because many of the procedures and techniques used in mounting a bass, such as cutting and skinning, will be the same with other fish.

The tools used to skin a bass vary from one taxidermist to the next, but the ones that I have shown here *(figure 1-1)* should make the job relatively easy, even for the novice. They are, from left to right; small sharp knife such as a pocket knife (we ground a #9 dental spatula into the small knife shown); a small scalpel, for cleaning the eye sockets; a special Diems skinning knife, obtainable at taxidermy supply houses but not a necessity (a pocket knife can be substituted). The Diem tool is serrated on the edges and does a fine job that will eliminate many unnecessary cuts. The scissors are floral shears that can be purchased from a florist supplier and they also have a serrated edge which makes cutting easier. Finally, there is the sponge which we use to mop up the water and blood that accumulates on the skinning table and a small pan to wash your hands in.

Before starting the actual skinning, wash the entire fish with a hard spray from a garden hose nozzle. Spray from the head toward the tail at an angle so that no scales become dislodged. The slime that is on most fish will come off easily if the fish has been frozen first.

STEP 1

With the shears, cut the fins off the back side of the fish. This is the side of the fish that will not be shown and the side from which we will work. Insert the knife behind the gill bone joint and start a shallow cut just under the skin *(figure 1-2)* moving towards the tail. Continue cutting along the center of the fish holding the finger within 1/4" of the tip of the knife. This keeps the knife from digging too deeply into the meat. Approach the tail keeping the knife centered and stop just at the junction of the scales and the fin rays *(figure 1-3 & 1-4)*.

Now, starting at the front of the throat, right under the gill, make a cut with your knife that extends under and around the gill to the very top *(figure 1-5)*. Cut the heavy bone just in back of the gill with the shears *(figure 1-6)*. Insert the scissors close up under the skin behind the gill and snip off the heavy bone that is there *(figure 1-7)*, then reverse the scissors and make the same cut in the opposite direction *(figure 1-8)*.

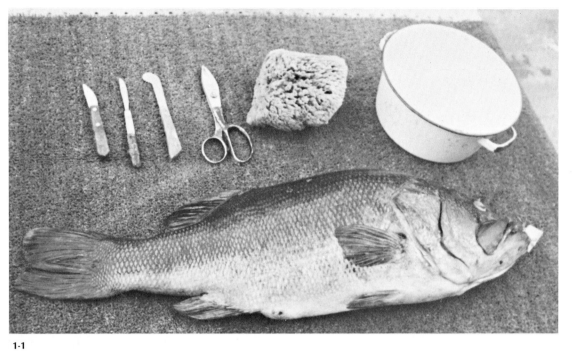

1-1

1-2

1-3

1-4

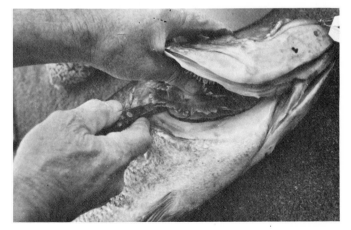

1-5

1-6

1-8

1-7

1-9

STEP 2

Begin separating the skin from the meat by inserting the skinning tool or pocket knife under the skin in the incision behind the gill *(figure 1-9)*, and starting a slow, steady paring motion. Be sure to separate the body meat from the skin at the very beginning because it will be harder to make the separation as you move down the fish. Hold the skin up and put tension on it with your other hand as you move down the fish *(figure 1-10)*. Be careful not to bend the skin too sharply or the scales on the "show" side of the fish will flip off. Slip the skinning knife further up into the skin as you move toward the tail. The knife should be touching the fin rays as you push it further up toward the back *(figure 1-11)*. Some meat will probably be left on the skin as you get closer to the tail. You may have trouble with this on fish that have been frozen for a long time. Get all the meat off that you can on the first skinning, because it will save you a lot of time later.

As the skinning progresses and the tail is reached, caution should be used in turning the skin at this finishing point. The front side scales will pop off very easily here *(figure 1-12)*. Pull the knife up snug with the base of the tail rays and stop.

1-10

STEP 3

Skin the lower side of the fish in the same manner *(figure 1-13)*. As the skin is removed on and around the belly, be careful and work very close to the skin. The skin sticks very tightly here and it will take more pressure from the knife to part it *(figure 1-14)*

If you hold your hand on the other side of the skin, you can pull the skin gently as you cut.

1-11

1-12

1-13

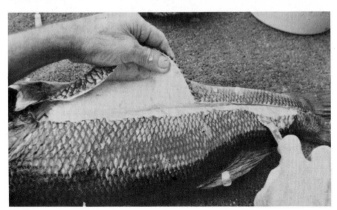

1-14

STEP 4

The next series of steps involve cutting the bones that run into the body of the fish. With the end of the scissors, start snipping the tail rays, one at a time *(figure 1-15)*. The meat must be removed to the very end of the tail, otherwise, after the mount dries, there will be a sunken place at this point. Cut all the way across to the other side of the tail and separate it from the body *(figure 1-16)*. If you hold your hand on the other side of the skin, you can feel the tip of the scissors when making the final separation.

Cut the fin rays at the place where they run into the body *(figure 1-17)*. It is always a good idea to hold your hand under the back and feel where the tip of the scissors are cutting. Work your way forward until the fin is loose. This cut should be made about 1/8 inch away from the skin *(figure 1-18)* .

Cut the two dorsal fins in the same way. Keep working and snipping along the fin line up the back *(figure 1-19)*, and after all of these bones have been cut, continue cutting with the scissors as far up into the head as the scissors will reach. Carefully snip the pelvic fins loose *(figure 1-20)*, leaving only the throat and backbone to disconnect.

1-15

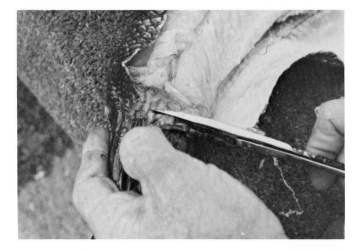

1-16

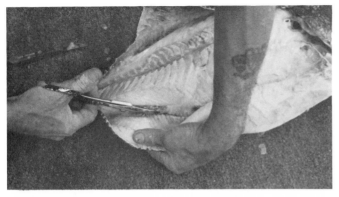

1-17

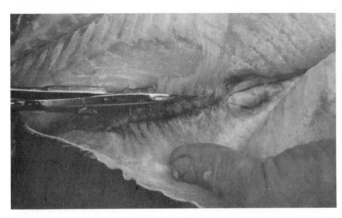

1-18

1-19

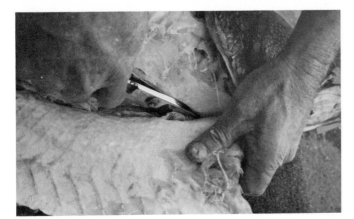

1-20

STEP 5

With your fingers, pry and separate the throat skin from the meat *(figure 1-21)*. With your fingers clear, snip the throat loose *(figure 1-22)*. Ease the meat back and cut the rest of the meat away from the pelvic fin. With the skinning tool, work all of the meat away from the skin *(figure 1-23)*.

1-21

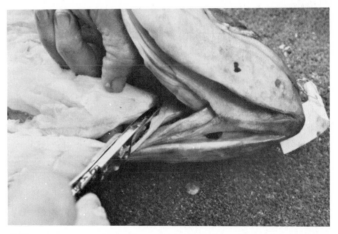

1-22

1-23

STEP 6

Starting at the base of the tail, unhook the skin from the body. There will be a tough muscle at the very base of the fin, and care must be exercised to keep from knocking off scales *(figure 1-24)*. Hold tension on the skin as you work it clear, and work forward, rolling the skin at a slight angle.

As you approach the anus, notice how much tension is on the skin. Keep it tight but don't pull too hard. There will be a tough layer here and care should be taken not to burst the abdominal cavity. It is better to use a little care here than to have to come back and clean off more meat later *(figure 1-25)*. Working up the middle is quite simple and here again you should try to get as much meat off the skin as possible.

The last of the skinning takes place at the head. When the bone is hit, work the skinning tool around it until all of the meat is hanging free. Cut through the shoulder bones and use the scissors to clean off whatever meat is left *(figure 1-26)*. After this has been taken care of, cut the remaining bone in the center of the fish *(figure 1-27)*.

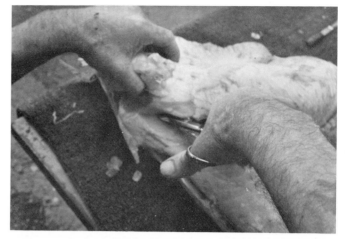

1-26

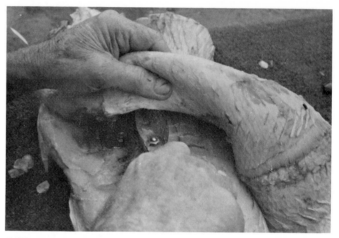

1-27

STEP 7

With the scissors just behind the gills, cut through the esophagus and meat, removing all that you can, until the backbone is reached *(figure 1-28)*. Thrust the scissors sharply against the backbone and apply a hard snapping motion to separate the bone. Cut all of the clinging meat away from the skin that remains and with a twisting motion, pull the meat from the skin *(figure 1-29)*.

1-24

1-25

1-28

Slip the scissors up beside the shoulder bones and the backbone *(figure 1-30)* and with hard downward strokes, separate both bone and meat. Do the same thing on the opposite side and with a twisting motion, pull this middle section out like an apple core *(figure 1-31)*. Continue working in the head section with the scissors, cutting all of the meat out that you can. Use a knife or scalpel when necessary and continue cleaning out the meat from the head.

STEP 8

Cut the base of the pectoral fin close to the hide *(figure 1-32)* and work the surplus meat away from the base of all fins *(figure 1-33)*. With the scissors, cut away the bone bases, and all hanging meat until a clean neat area is left *(figure 1-34)*. Next tape a sharp knife and begin cleaning all surplus meat off the skin *(figure 1-35)*. The fish in the photos was purposely left somewhat unclean to show the clinging meat and what it might look like to the beginner. I want to stress that the fish can be cleaned almost perfectly the first time if care is taken. The time it will save you is well worth the extra effort.

1-29

1-32

1-30

1-33

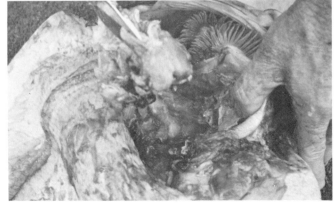

1-31

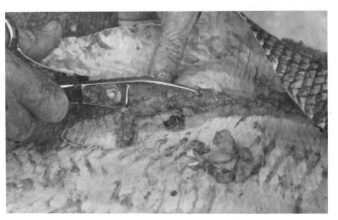

1-34

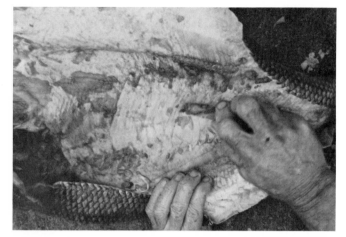

1-35

STEP 9

Insert a scalpel or knife down the side of the eye and lift it out *(figures 1-36 and 1-37)*. Slide the scalpel into the eye socket and cut away all of the meat *(figure 1-38)*. Pull the meat out with your fingers, making sure to get it all *(figure 1-39)*. If the eye socket is not clean, and free of meat, it will shrink in the drying process and cause the mount to look bad. When this is completed, you are ready to pickle the fish.

1-36

1-37

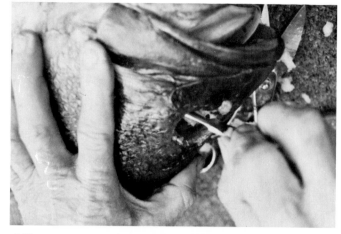

1-38

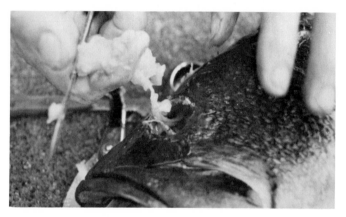

1-39

Pickling The Fish

Mix a solution of saturated borax. This is a water softener used in washing clothes that can be purchased at almost any store in large quantities at chemical supply houses or at taxidermy supply houses. One brand is 20 Mule Borax.

To make the solution, mix a handful in about two gallons of water. If any settles to the bottom you have used too much borax. It will not hurt the solution but you are wasting your money. Immerse the skin in this solution and let it sit overnight or at least four to six hours. I like for the meat at the base of the fins to take on a pale white color rather than a pink color. This tells me that the solution has penetrated deep into the skin. Another reason for the overnight immersion is that some fish have a slight odor that this overnight soaking will drive off.

Oily and Smelly Fish

Some fish such as the lake trouts, wahoos, mackerel, and many of the salmons have very oily skin and some will smell to high heaven, especially large redfish and drum. By immersing the head portion in Solox (denatured wood alcohol) for three or four hours, you can get rid of the smell, and the solution will pull the oil out.

THE HOLLOW MOUNT METHOD

Of all the methods that we will cover in this book, it would be unfair not to rate them as to which has the greatest potential, lowest cost of production, speed, and ease with which it is taught. We mount many and various species and I have tried a lot of methods through the years. Considering time, quality and all of the other factors mentioned above, we invariably come back to our hollow mount method.

The internal structure is very strong, which gives the mount a sturdy foundation. This is a great asset when shipping fish to customers and when mounting bass, a fast system can be set up to handle a large volume. Another good thing about this system is that it works well on four and five foot fish such as barracuda, dolphin and also small fish such as brim and crappie. Fish mounted in the hollow mount method dry very fast, since the inside is filled with dry sawdust, only the skin and the thin liner get wet. The head section, of course, is always the last to dry. The beginner may be a little slow at first in visualizing the right shape of the fish and then applying it to the mount, but the other methods will probably give him the same problem.

You will notice that I have included many photos in this book, where an explanation may be sufficient, but it was my experience when I picked up taxidermy "how to" books several years ago, some thirty three to be exact, that I would like to have seen several more illustrations or photos, of which there never seemed to be quite enough.

The author must have thought that, I was more brilliant than I thought I was.

This method is not simply for the amateurs, but for whoever wants a quality mount and a method using materials that are readily available. Our Hollow Mount Methods fills the bill on all counts.

Mounting Large Fish

Fish up to five or six feet are generally mounted with the hollow mount method. This includes dolphin, barracuda, redfish, and many others. The larger salt water fish are sometimes very oily and require the fiberglass process. This is discussed at length in the section on fiberglass mounts.

Drying Rooms

After many fish are mounted, drying becomes a problem. Many taxidermists simply put the fish on a shelf and let the elements do the work for them. In our shop, we have a room with many shelves on it where we stack fish and keep a heater and a slightly blowing fan running at all times. This speeds the drying time from 3 to 5 days on an average bass. It also insures that the fish are bone dry when you take them out and prepare them for painting.

Preparation and Tools

After you have skinned the fish it has soaked in the borax solution, take it out and spray it off with water. Hang it up to let the excess water drip off *(figure 2-1)*.

The tools needed for this method are as follows *(figure 2-2)*.

— A Bostich P3 Stapling pliers - other brands will do but we have found that this one will clean up easier and is less of a headache to maintain.
— An Arrow T10 Tacker using ⅜ inch staples.
— Three inch upholstering pins, used to hold the fins in place.
— Any kind of medium heavy scissors.
— Any kind of medium heavy scissors.
— Jumbo Gem Clips, used to card the fins.
— Popsicle sticks, broken in half, used on the tail to hold it straight.

Joint compound will be the main ingredient in a mache compound which we will make. This product can be purchased at most building supply houses. With this basic substance, many formulas can be made *(figure 2-3)*.

The next ingredient is sawdust. Use the finest that you can find, from a band saw or around a sawmill where the fines spill out. Note the texture of the two ingredients in figure 2-4.

Mix about half and half of each substance in a dry container. Next, using a plastic mixing bowl, put water in first, then add the mixture and mix until it is somewhat stiff *(figure 2-5)*.

The stuffing stick is one of the most important items. You can make this by tapering the ends of a round wooden dowel, 1/2" or 3/4" thick and twelve to fourteen inches long. A grinder is helpful in doing this but it can be carved by hand if one is not available. Taper one end fairly blunt, with a long taper on the other end. This is important when it comes to packing the sawdust into the fish *(figure 2-6)*.

2-2

2-1

STEP 1

Staple the cut in the esophagus closed to eliminate sawdust escaping when you begin packing the mount.

With your finger, poke some mache into the eye socket. You may need something to work it down into the back section of the eye *(figure 2-7)*. Use some newspaper or old phone book pages and press it into the mache *(figure 2-8)*. This will help to press the mache into place and give the front of the eye a smooth appearance.

The next thing you will need is a piece of open weave burlap larger than the whole fish skin *(figure 2-9)*. You can use old potato sacks or buy this kind of burlap by the yard. Taxidermy supply houses also carry burlap.

STEP 2

Lay the fish down on the cloth and use the skin to make a pattern for the liner which will go in the fish *(figure 2-10)*. Cut the burlap along the outer edge of the fish, al-

lowing an inch or more extra *(figure 2-11)*. It is always a good idea to leave extra at the base of the tail to insure a firm tight tail *(figure 2-12)*. On a "pot bellied" fish, drop down about two inches extra to accommodate the fullness of the belly and then continue to the tail *(figure 2-13)*. One advantage of this method is that each fish is mounted to its exact skin size, and all of them will have an individual shape. Remove the fish and turn the burlap over, laying it flat. Later we will cover it with mache and place it in the fish.

2-5

2-6

2-7

2-4

2-3

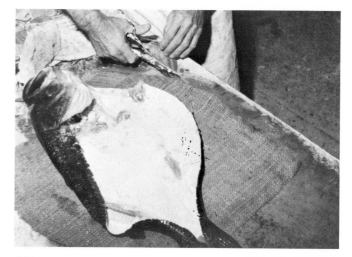

2-8

2-9

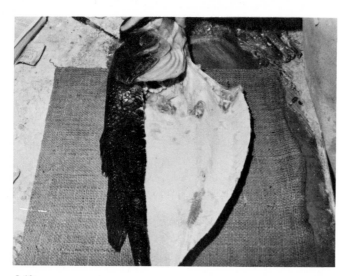

2-10

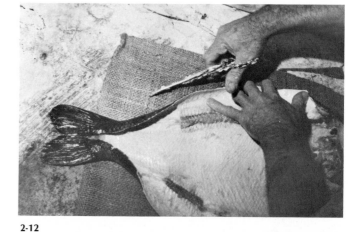

2-11

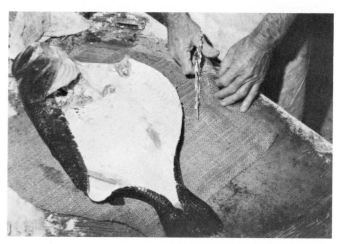

2-12

2-13

STEP 3

Smear mache into the bony sections of the head and smooth it out with your fingers. Do this along the dorsal where the bones were snipped off and at the base of the anal fin *(figures 2-14 and 2-15)*. A small amount at the base of the tail will insure a snug fit *(figure 2-16)*.

STEP 4

In this next step, you will need some tow or excelsior *(figure 2-17)*. Take a small wad of this and dip it into the mache bucket getting some of the mache on one side of the wad *(figure 2-18)*. Insert this into the head section, forcing it in with your fingers to fill all of the void space

2-14

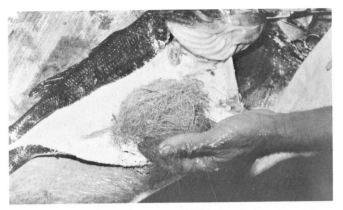

2-17

2-15

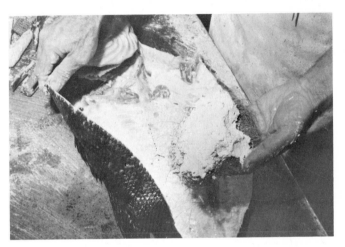

2-18

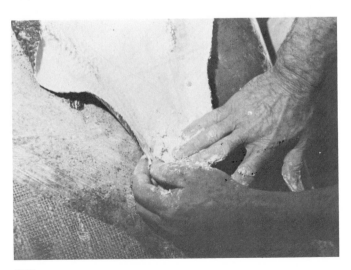

2-16

(figure 2-19). It is important to firm this up, otherwise the head will develop a sag and will not look right after the sawdust is packed in. Work a little more of the mache into the tow from the back of the head then check to see if the upper part of the head is smooth from the outside.

STEP 5

Take a full handful of mache and put it in the middle of the cloth. Start from the center and work the mache to the outside edges, pressing the mache into the fibers of the burlap (figure 2-20). This takes some practice because sometimes the mache comes off in your hand as fast as you smooth it on. Continue spreading from the center until the entire piece is covered (figures 2-21 and 2-22). The layer doesn't have to be very thick, but the larger the fish, the thicker the coat should be. I generally add some thickness in the center and near the belly section as a safeguard. The part at the tail can be thinnest because it is narrow and will not receive much stress. The cloth is now finished and ready to be laid into the fish.

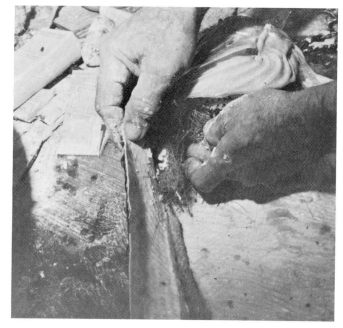

2-19

2-22

2-20

STEP 6

Lay open the bass skin and have it ready to receive the cloth *(figure 2-23)*. It will save time if you lay the cloth in the correct position without having to pick it back up or move it around. Snug the cloth up tight into the throat area and work it neatly into place. Notice in the photos how it fits all the way up into the fish, without any wrinkles *(figure 2-24)*.

Trim away any surplus cloth at the tail section, and we are now ready to begin the fitting process.

It is important that we make the head firm, and this joining together of the cloth and the tow that is packed in the head is a critical junction. To make a good fit, use one hand to press from the inside and the other to feel what is happening on the outside of the skin *(figure 2-25)*. Once the head is tucked in, check the throat section and tuck it in tight against the esophagus *(figure 2-26)*.

2-21

2-23

2-24

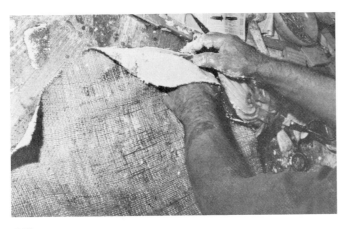

2-25

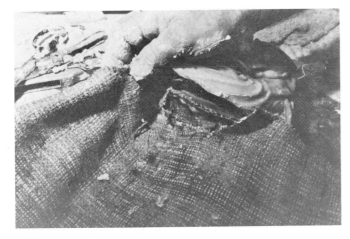

2-26

Continue this procedure down one side. As the liner is fitted, the surplus burlap will hang out *(figure 2-29).* Trim this off and continue *(figure 2-30).*

2-27

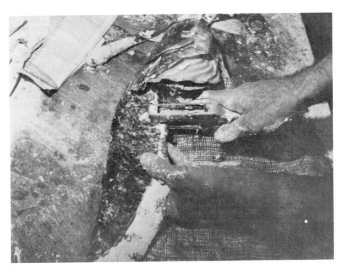

2-28

2-29

Follow the bone line and press the cloth into place with your fingers *(figure 2-27).*

STEP 7

Hold the cloth tightly against the skin and take all of the slack out of the skin by pulling the cloth to the rear with your fingers. Try to get the liner as tight as possible against the skin. The first staple is very important. If any slack is in the head section, it is hard to work out later *(figure 2-28).*

2-30

2-32

When you come to the upper middle section, check from the front and make sure no slack is in the skin before proceeding. Always check and recheck as you are stapling. You should be at a point now where you can trim away all of the extra cloth, leaving only a small margin which you can trim away later *(figure 2-31)*. Finish stapling all the way to the tail and trim away the surplus cloth *(figure 2-32)*.

STEP 8

Start at the lower section of the tail now and begin stapling toward the belly, using the twisting motion to press the cloth tight against the skin *(figure 2-33)*. Be careful when you reach the belly and use extra care in making sure the cloth goes into the pocket that forms "pot bellied" bass *(figure 2-34)*. Sometimes at this point, we will cut a small three or four inch slit into the cloth and force another piece of burlap into that slit to give the belly more fullness. Some customers are fussy about this and you can add fullness with this little trick. If you use care though, and work closely, this can be achieved without cutting the slit.

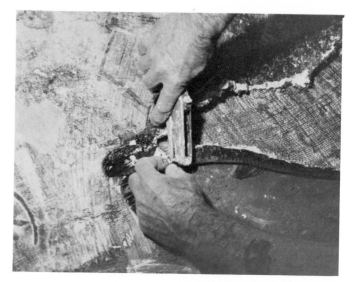

2-33

2-31

2-34

The Pot Bellied Bass - Comments

In figure 2-35, you will see a variety of bass which, like people, are all different. Many customers will swear that they brought in a fish like #1 in the photo, and yet they may have brought you a #5. What do you do?

The only place you can get enough slack in the skin to add this extra bulk, is to leave a gap in the back and allow the skin to come around to the front side to make up the difference. With the hollow mount method this can be done by allowing the burlap to be used in place of the edge of the skin. In the system using foam bodies, use a larger form and leave a gap in the back. There are a number of ways to do this but certain problems can occur. For one thing, the scales of a fish are a certain size and have a slight curve that is in contour with its original shape. If this is changed too radically, over a short period of time, the scale will begin raising up. Secondly, if distorted too drastically, the anus will appear on the side of the fish instead of in the middle where it belongs. The fins will also have to be positioned in such a way that will make the fish out of round. I try to strike a happy balance with this problem, and if a fellow wants a super belly, I explain the options and then give him what he wants.

The bass you see in figure 2-36 is an example of how the size of the belly can be misjudged. When hanging, all of the gut of the fish have sunken to the lower part, causing the belly to protrude more than normal. Looking at the vent fin, you will see a sunken section. When the fish is mounted this place will fill back out and it will appear

that some of the belly has been removed-it has not. The rest of the fish has been filled and it will appear that some of the girth is gone. Knowing this may help you in dealing with some of your customers.

2-36

2-35

STEP 9

After the last staple has been placed at the shoulderbone, fitting the throat comes next *(figure 2-37)*. If the throat has been skinned out properly, the layer of skin can be extended and the cloth tucked into it. Tuck it into the very corner making sure there are no wrinkles in the front *(figure 2-38)*. Place one staple in the front of the throat and continue back to the left until you reach the shoulder bone *(figure 2-39)*. The liner is now fitted and in place.

STEP 10

Smear mache onto the burlap liner, pressing it into the cloth *(figure 2-40)*. Be sure to cover the cloth all the way out to the edges with an equal thickness. Work it around the throat and up against the meat of the head. The belly section should be covered a little thicker than the rest *(figure 2-41)*. Figure 2-42 shows the section where the cloth can be split from the inside and extra added to give the mount a fuller belly. Figure 2-43 shows where

2-37

2-40

2-38

2-41

2-39

2-42

this cut should be made from the inside.

Bring the edges together at the base of the tail and staple them together, moving up about one inch *(figure 2-44)*.

STEP 11

Tuck a tight wad of tow into the throat and snug it back against the esophagus *(figure 2-45)*. The tow should be almost in place when the collar is brought together *(figure 2-46)*. Hold the collar or shoulder bones together tightly and staple them together *(figure 2-47)*. Several staples may be necessary to secure the collar.

Pull the bottom gill up and over the bone and hold it in place while you staple it to the shoulder bone with several staples *(figures 2-48 and 2-49)*.

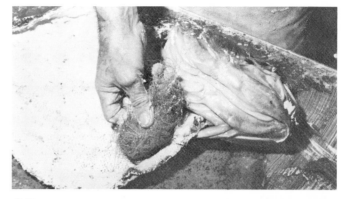

2-45

2-46

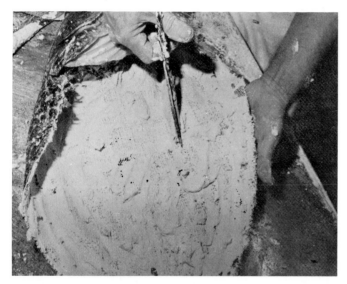

2-43

2-47

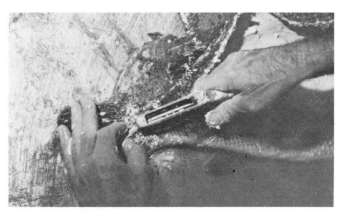

2-44

2-48

2-49

STEP 12

Fill a small plastic bowl with sawdust that is not too coarse. A Tupperware cereal bowl works well because it can be bent and the sawdust funneled into the cavity *(figure 2-50)*. Fill toward the tail until the entire fish is loosely filled. Hold the skin up with your hands and begin forcing sawdust into all the loose areas *(figure 2-51)*. Firm it up as much as you can with your fingers before using the stuffing stick.

Continue to add sawdust as it is packed in. The first place you will need the stuffing stick is at the tail section *(figure 2-52)*. Hold the skin with one hand and pack the sawdust whenever necessary with the stuffing stick. Firm up the head section, keeping one hand on the outside of the skin to feel the shape *(figure 2-53)*. Check closely for soft spots and direct the stick and additional sawdust to those areas until they are shaped and firm.

2-51

2-52

2-50

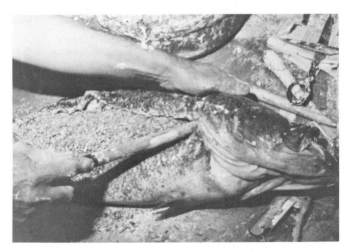

2-53

STEP 13

Put a few more staples from the collar bone back a couple of inches, then go back to the tail and continue filling and stapling toward the belly *(figure 2-54)*. When you are about midway, fill and shape the belly *(figure 2-55)*. Add a few more staples, narrowing the gap that is left open to several inches *(figure 2-56)*. Apply firm pressure when developing the belly pocket. Use the long tapered end of the stuffing stick and add sawdust until the desired shape of the belly is achieved. Add as much sawdust as necessary to fill out the belly and any soft places completely *(figure 2-57)*.

2-57

In the place where the wooden mounting block will be, it is important that you add more sawdust or a soft spot will appear on the front side. The point is to leave just enough room to receive the wooden block. For an eight to ten pound bass, we use a piece of 3/4" exterior grade plywood with the upper and lower edges tapered *(figure 2-58)*.

2-54

STEP 14

Insert the lower edge of the block first *(figure 2-59)*. Then press the block all of the way in, pulling the upper part of the skin over it *(figure 2-60)*.

Smear a wad of mache under the upper and lower sides of the skin on top of the block *(figure 2-61)*. Pull the skin up on the lower side and staple it with five or six staples *(figure 2-62)*. Pull the skin down from the upper side and staple it in the same manner *(figure 2-63)*.

2-55

2-58

2-56

2-59

2-60

2-61

2-62

2-63

STEP 15

To fill the throat, raise the gill and place a wad of mache under the gill in the cavity *(figure 2-64)*. Use a piece of newspaper against the mache to press it firmly into place. With a spatula, slick the mache down *(figure 2-65)*. Work it until you have a nice smooth shape. The fish is now mounted and ready to be cleaned up *(figure 2-66)*.

2-64

2-65

2-66

STEP 16

Move the fish and clean up your work table first. With a hose, spray the fish clean (figure 2-67) being careful not to wash any of the mache out of the seam in the back.

2-67

STEP 17

With a wooden paddle, carefully tap out all of the bumps and irregularities, getting the mount in its proper shape (figure 2-68). There are usually some places around the head that need some attention. Move down the seam patting the mount into shape as you go. Make the tail lean and toward the flat side. The fish should be sprayed off again before proceeding.

Hold the fish by the spiney dorsal fins and paddle out a slight wedge, tapering it toward the middle (figure 2-69). Most taxidermists tend to leave a rounded shoulder which is not exactly right. It should be patted down some.

Shape the front and double-check for any places that may need attention. At this stage the fish is totally pliable and ready to be shaped.

2-68

2-69

STEP 18 CARDING THE FINS

Before the mount is shaped, we must get the fins into their final shape. We do this by carding the fins.

Fin cards can be made several ways. Some taxidermists make them from milk cartons and others use a fine hardware cloth cut to the fin size and place a plastic card on top. There are many combinations and most taxidermists use different methods.

For my fin cards I use a paper board called printers blank .030, which can be bought at paper companies and cut this into cards that are right for the size fish I am mounting. Next I fill a five gallon bucket with Gulf 40 parafin wax which has a low melting point. I have a wire basket that will fit into the bucket and a wire bail to lift it out with. I melt the wax in the bucket with a Coleman stove and bring it to a boil. The wire basket is then filled with the cards and lowered into the boiling wax. If you have plans to mount a lot of fish, it would be worth your while to take your paper board to a printer and let them cut it to the sizes you need with their paper shears.

Let the cards stay in the boiling wax until no more bubbles come up, usually about five minutes. Raise the basket and let the wax drain. Dump the cards into a cardboard box and they are ready to use. The wax impregnated cards will not stick to the fins and you don't have to worry about wax coming off and getting on the fish to mess up your painting later. We have used this method for many years with no bad results and the cards can be used over and over again.

To card the gills, place one of the gill cover cards on top and one underneath the gill. Pull the gill its full length, hold it in place (figure 2-70), and slip a jumbo size gem clip into the cards. Use several gem clips to hold the cards on the gills. I never use less than three (figure 2-71).

2-70

2-71

STEP 19

You will need a couple of wedge shaped pieces of balsa wood or pine for props when you get ready to give the fish its curve (figure 2-72). With one hand on the body of the fish, lift up from underneath (figure 2-73). When you have the mount curved the way you want it, apply a final, slight, upward push. Wet your hands now and rub the entire fish down to make sure that it was not mashed anywhere while you were shaping the mount.

2-72

2-73

STEP 20

You can now put on the rest of the fin cards. Spread the vent fins evenly and naturally (figure 2-74). Slip the top card onto the fin and gem clip it (figure 2-75). Repeat this on all of the fins, including the tail. At the tail, slip a broken popsicle stick under the edge of the top and bottom of the fin (figure 2-76). This will keep it looking natural and straight and keep it from drooping as it dries. Under the lower vent fin stick in a long upholstering pin to hold the fin out and up. Do this behind the other fins including the tail fin.

Use pieces of cardboard for gill spacers (figure 2-77). Raise the gills and insert these between each gill (figure

2-78). Adjust them to suit yourself. Some people raise the gills higher than others.

STEP 21

To complete the mounting process, gently press the tongue into the bottom of the mouth *(figure 2-79).* Lowering the tongue will give the head a larger appearance. Finally check the fish one more time to make sure that all irregularities are out. If you are satisfied, the fish is now ready for drying *(figure 2-80).*

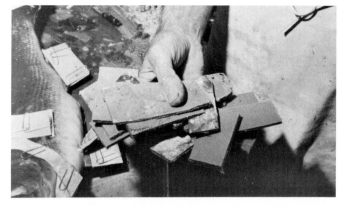

2-77

2-74

2-78

2-75

2-79

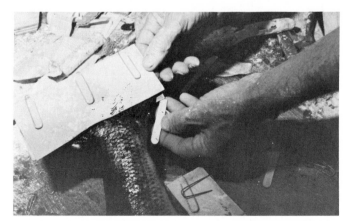

2-76

2-80

THE FISH FILL METHOD

This method has become popular in taxidermy in the last few years because of new and lightweight aggregate materials that have come on the market recently. These materials are used in industry and agriculture and are an excellent ingredient for another (similar to the one used in the Hollow Mount Method) mache type material which can be used as a filler to make lightweight mounts. Although there are some good commercial grades of pre-mixed fillers which can be bought, we will give you a formula which works well and is easy to make. The fish fill method is fast and simple and in general, one that is hard to go wrong with.

For this method you will need a tacker, a grip staple, excelsior, and a mixing bowl to make the mache in. You will also need a small block of wood to insert for the mounting attachment. To make the filler, you will need perlite and plaster as shown in figure 3-1. You will also need joint cement in this mixture.

STEP 1

After you have skinned the fish and washed it, make the filler. To do this, fill the mixing bowl with about one inch of water and begin adding joint cement (figure 3-2). To this add coarse perlite (figure 3-3). If the mixture is too thin, you may have to add more of each, the purpose is to make a firm stiff mixture. Sawdust can be added to this

3-1

3-2

3-3

3-5

mixture as a filler for a less expensive grade. Mix this thoroughly with your hands. If it is too watery it will make the mount sag and it will not shape up well in the final steps *(figure 3-4)*.

STEP 3

Smear some of this mixture onto a small handful of excelsior *(figure 3-5)*. Raise the gill cover and pack this into the head cavity with your fingers *(figure 3-6)*, firming the head up well.

STEP 4

Pull the skin together at the base of the tail and staple it tightly with several staples *(figure 3-7)*. Use the stapler to connect the shoulder bones as they were before they were cut *(figure 3-8)*, checking to make sure that the staples hold securely. Pull the gill cover over on top of this bone and staple the gill to it *(figures 3-9 and 3-10)*. Notice in figure 3-11 the point at which these staples were attached.

3-6

3-4

3-7

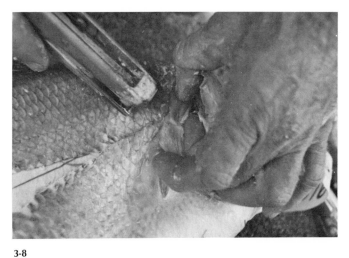

3-8

3-9

3-10

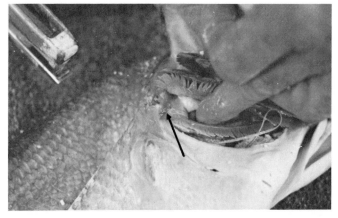

3-11

STEP 5

Begin adding the filler to the middle of the fish. Press the material from the center out to the edges *(figure 3-12)*. Move to the tail section and pack it firmly, stapling as you proceed forward *(figure 3-13)*. We use the stapler because it is faster; however, a needle and thread can be used.

3-12

3-13

STEP 6

Add more of the filler to the belly, stretching the stomach as much as you want. Also fill the head completely at this point, all of the way back to the shoulder *(figure 3-14)*.

Continue stapling from the tail, pulling the skin together tightly to receive the staples *(figure 3-15)*. Add more filler as you go. You might find it harder to pack the material as you approach the belly, but keep the fish firm as you staple it up *(figure 3-16)*. When you have a three to four inch opening left, pack the mixture with small whiffs of excelsior in the areas that need it *(figure 3-17)*. Fill the opening until it is tight and not spongy *(figure 3-18)*. Check the front of the fish for any loose areas as well as the back and tail.

3-16

3-14

3-17

3-15

3-18

STEP 7

When you are ready to place the block in the mount, smear the exposed excelsior with the filler. This extra filler helps seat the block and makes a tighter fit. Three quarter inch exterior plywood makes a good block, but any type of wood that holds a screw well will do.

Push the block into the opening and pull the other edge of the skin over it *(figure 3-19)*. Work more filler all around the block and staple both edges of the skin onto it *(figure 3-20)*. With the block in place fill the eye sockets with the mixture, pressing small pieces of paper into the sockets to fill out all of the void space.

3-19

3-20

3-21

STEP 8

Wash off both sides of the fish, but be careful not to wash out any of the filler around the seam. Try using a hose pipe, and make quick passes over the fish with the water.

STEP 9

Open the gill and check to make sure that the throat is filled. Add some scraps of newspaper to fill it out more if necessary.

Place a wax card under the lower gill cover, spread it out to its full length, and clip the card to it. *(figure 3-21)*. Card the top gill cover the same way and slip some cardboard gill spacers between the gills to separate them *(figure 3-22)*.

STEP 10

Turn the fish over on its show side and look for any flaws or sections that need repairs. Use a wooden paddle and lightly pat the mount to work it into the desired shape. The fish will dent easily at this stage so work with a light touch. Work the back into a slight wedge bringing the mount to its final shape *(figure 3-23)*. It helps to wet your hands and rub them over the fish to detect any bad places which you otherwise might miss.

3-22

3-23

STEP 11

In the final steps, proceed as discussed in the Hollow Mount Method. Hold the fish in the center with one hand and raise the tail carefully for the bend. A wedge shaped piece of wood is used to hold the tail up. Raise the head in the same manner and place a block of wood under it also *(figure 3-24)*.

STEP 12

Card all of the fins and gill covers *(figure 3-25)* with the waxed cards. Give the end section of the tail an upward push and you will notice that this loosens it up, making it possible to put the tail in any desired position *(figure 3-26)*. After you have the tail in place check the fish one more time to make sure it is nice and smooth. If you find any dents, get them out now. The fish is now ready for drying.

3-25

3-24

3-26

THE EXCELSIOR CORE METHOD FOR MOUNTING FISH

The Excelsior Core Method is probably one of the simplest of all methods of fish mounting. There are many advantages for the person doing the work. Supplies are easy to get for this method and they are generally cheap. In addition to this, the size of the fish can be exaggarated and made to look larger.

This method is especially good on bass and for those people who want a "pot bellied" bass. Using the Excelsior Core Method, they can have one as large as they want.

This method is fast too. For the beginner it does not take a lot of skill to turn out a good mount, but like other methods it will only be as good as the effort put forth. I would like to emphasize that this is not an amateur method. It is being used in some of the largest commercial shops in the country.

The materials needed are shown in figure 4-1. They are, from left to right, a tacker, scissors, knife, a wooden block, strips of newspaper, a long straight needle and thread, popsicle sticks, cotton twine or other winding cord, and excelsior or wood wood as it is commonly called.

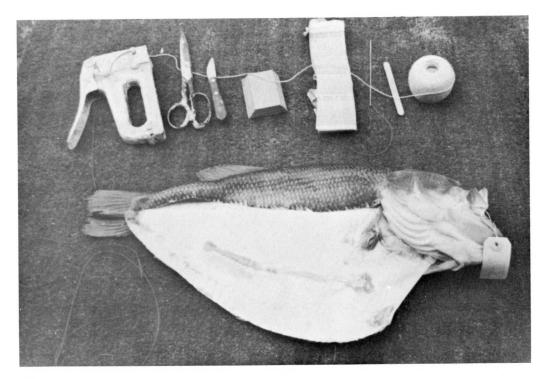

4-1

STEP 1

With a large handful of excelsior, start loosely wrapping it roughly into the shape of the fish body *(figure 4-2)*. Mash the material and wind the string tighter *(figure 4-3)*. As you tighten up, begin to shape it with your hands, continuing to wrap more string around it. Place the core body beside the fish skin and compare them to see what is necessary to make it look like the meat that came out of the fish *(figure 4-4)*.

STEP 2

Continue the winding and as a better shape begins to emerge, check the fit in the skin to see if you need more excelsior *(figure 4-5)*. Add excelsior to any areas that need it, and be careful not to get the fish too flat *(figure 4-6)*. Refit the core and check the shoulder joint to make sure this area fits *(figure 4-7)*. The tail must also be a close fit or there will be a bulging look *(figure 4-8)*.

4-2

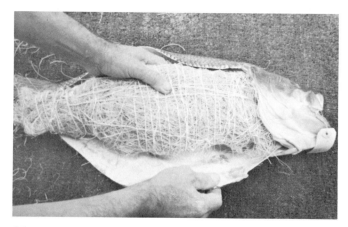

4-5

4-3

4-6

4-4

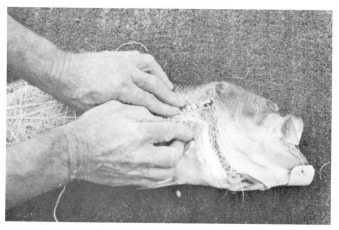

4-7

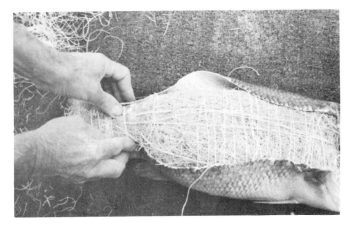

4-8

STEP 3

If you want the fish to be "Pot Bellied" this is the time to make it. Working a ball of excelsior the size you want the belly to be. Remember that the excelsior will pack quite a bit, so it is a good idea to make it a little larger than it needs to be *(figure 4-9)*. The core body should be ready for the fish when you have finished this *(figure 4-10)*.

4-9

4-10

STEP 4

Using the same mache that was discussed in chapter 2, smear it onto the skin and into the head cavity about a quarter of an inch thick *(figures 4-11 and 4-12)*. It is important to apply a good even coat all over. To place the block of wood in the core simply spread the excelsior with your hands, insert the block and wrap some string around the body to lock it in *(figure 4-13)*.

4-11

4-12

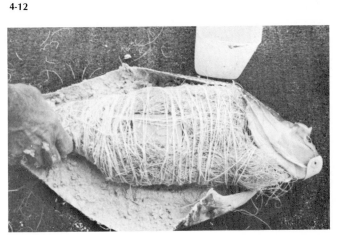

4-13

STEP 5

Place this into the skin and smear some of the mache into the core. This adds strength to the mount and takes the place of the mache that slips back off the edge of the skin after the sewing starts *(figure 4-14)*.

STEP 6

Put the first stitch just behind the belly toward the tail *(figure 4-15)*. Don't pull this stitch hard, but rather with your hands, draw the two edges of the skin as close as they need to be *(figure 4-16)*. If you pull this first stitch too hard you will simply pull the stitches out. Continue with a zig-zag stitch down the fish pulling and shaping the fish as each stitch is entered *(figure 4-17)*. As you near the tail it will get a little harder to stitch. Here you should shorten your stitch and mash the material a little harder *(figure 4-18)*. The last stitch in the tail is critical and should be pulled in snug and all the way together. After this tie a knot and cut the string.

4-16

4-17

4-14

4-18

4-15

STEP 7

Pull the shoulders together and put in a stitch *(figure 4-19)*. It is not necessary to pull it all the way together here; only if you want to. Sew down the back the same way the tail was done. Stitches can be wide and far apart. *(figure 4-20)*. The reason we are not showing a neat job with the stitches not brought all of the way together on the mount is because most customers are happier with a mount that looks bigger than the one they caught.

This is the best method for this type of mount. Just use your own judgment as we mentioned earlier and make the fish bellies as large as the heart desires.

shape the front of the belly *(figure 4-25)*. Be careful not to get the front too flat. Make it slightly rounded and the curve will enhance the mounts inner strength.

4-21

4-19

4-22

4-20

STEP 8

Note the bulges and the irregularities in the skin when the sewing is complete *(figure 4-21)*. On the mount in figure 4-22 there are some irregular shapes near the back and close to the head. Use a wooden paddle to lightly tap and shape the back and top into the way you want it *(figure 4-23)*. The mache liner shifts under the skin to enable this molding. Work around the belly and get it the way you want it.

Move to the front side and begin shaping the contour *(figure 4-24)*. Work the bone section of the head and

4-23

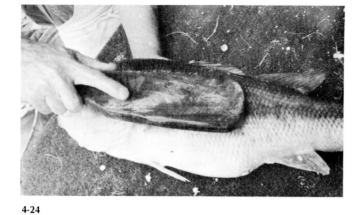

4-24

4-25

4-27

4-28

STEP 9

Fill the eye with mache *(figure 4-26),* and wash the excess mache and debris off the fish. Do this quick to keep from washing mache out of the seam *(figure 4-27).* Raise the gill and fill the throat with mache *(figure 4-28).* Fill the area around the upper side of the head and you are ready to card the fins.

For details on carding the fins, refer to Chapter Two, and follow the same procedure used in the Hollow Mount Method.

4-26

TAXIDERMY
SHOWCASE

A well shaped largemouth bass with a nice full belly.

The author finishing a group
of bass.

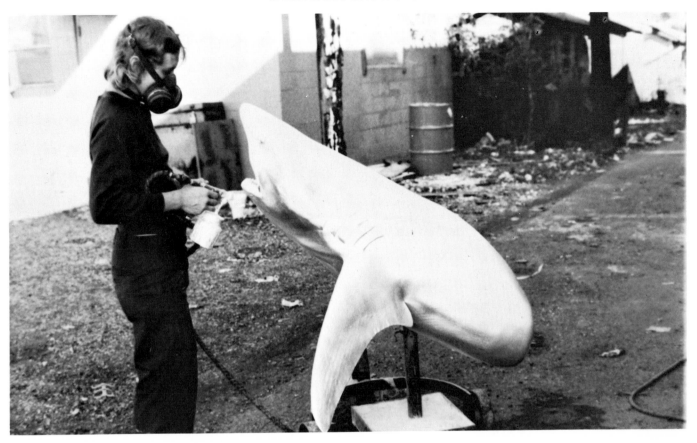

Bubba Phillips, finishing a large quarter mount head of a shark.

Leaping sailfish are a favorite mount in the Gulf area.

This 3¾ lb. redear sunfish would be a conversation piece on anyone's wall.

The author with a 48′ hammerhead shark.

A beautiful set of sunfish — left — 3¾ lb. redear sunfish, upper right — 4 lb. 6 oz. crappie, — lower 3¾ lb. bluegill brim.

This muskie makes a nice wall mount.

Northern Pike are a most sought out trophy and one of the main fish for the northern taxidermist.

Most catfish are reproduced, as their skins will not hold up to any mounting process.

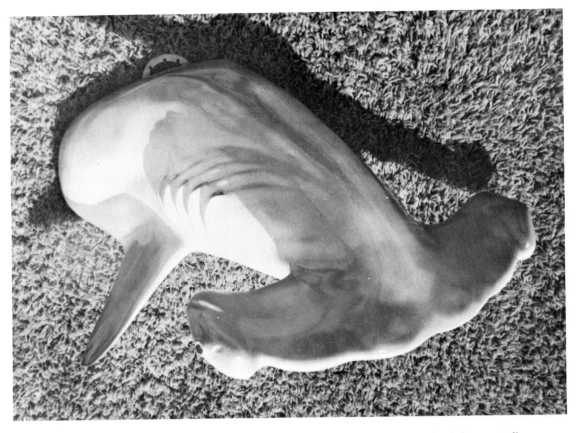

This quarter mount hammerhead was from a fish of about 125 lbs.

After the movie Jaws, we have mounted lots of these big boys. This one weighed about 200 lbs.

This is the first place winner crappie for the reproduction class at the Biloxi National Taxidermy Convention. This is our 4 lb. 6 oz. fish.

A mixed group of both skin mounts and reproductions in our showroom in Fairfield, Ala.

The saltwater Cobia makes a nice mount.

1947 World Record bream caught by Coke McKenzie at Ketona Lake, near Birmingham, Alabama. This record was beaten several years later by two ounces, but that fish was not preserved.

COKE McKENZIE, OF 3941 HALE AVENUE, BIRMINGHAM, WAS FISHING ONE NIGHT LAST APRIL 1947 WITH A POLE IN KETONA LAKE, NEAR BIRMINGHAM, USING RED WORMS FOR BAIT. A TUG ON HIS LINE WAS FOLLOWED BY THREE MINUTES OF BATTLING THAT LEFT COKE'S EYES POPPING WHEN HE FINALLY LANDED WHAT TURNED OUT TO BE THE WORLD'S LARGEST BLUEGILL BREAM. IT WEIGHED FOUR AND ONE-HALF POUNDS, WAS 15½ INCHES IN LENGTH, EIGHT INCHES IN DEPTH AND WAS THREE INCHES THICK. THE AGE OF THIS BREAM WAS NINE YEARS. IT WAS A TRUE BLUEGILL, DESPITE EFFORTS OF SOME TO MAKE IT A KISSIN'-COUSIN TO A WHALE. THE PREVIOUS RECOGNIZED WORLD'S RECORD HOLDER WAS A TWO-POUND 10 OUNCE BLUEGILL CAUGHT IN 1945 BY P. E. BROOCH AT SILVER LAKE, MICHIGAN.

The rainbow trout is so colorful that it has always been a trophy for the walls of sportsmen.

THE PRE-CAST FOAM BODY METHOD

In the last few years many taxidermy supply houses have developed foam fish bodies. These are usually well shaped and good fitting forms that give very desirable results. Foam bodies have become a great asset to the taxidermist and although all fish cannot be purchased, some of the companies have a fairly good selection. If a particular body does not fit exactly right, modifications with a wrasp are very easy to do.

The selection shown in figure 5-1 are for bass. Notice that they are very smooth and have good girths and contours. Those shown in figure 2 represent a good selection for the many trout that you will be called on to mount.

STEP 1

Before the actual mounting starts, I cut a square out of the back of the form where I will mount a block of wood. This is to anchor the screws into the panel of the finished mount (figure 5-3). I glue it in with some form of quick epoxy or a hot glue gun.

STEP 2

With a wood wrasp, knock off the burrs that came about from the molding process (figure 5-4), then sand this midline into the contour of the body (figure 5-5).

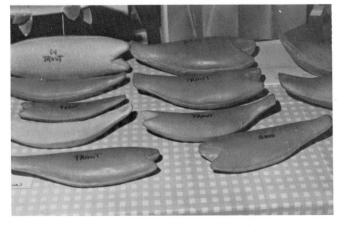

5-1

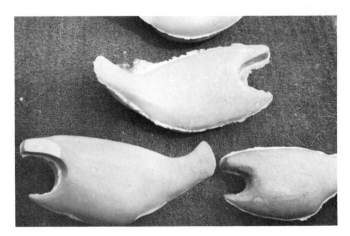

5-2

The materials needed besides the foam body are some excelsior, a tacker, sandpaper and mache. Refer to Chapter Two for making the mache.

5-3

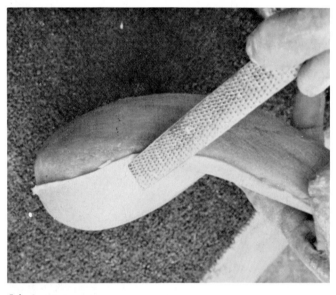

5-4

5-5

STEP 3

Lay the body into the skin and notice by the dotted lines where the bones of the anal fin and dorsal fins come on the bottom and top of the form *(figure 5-6)*. Use a pocket knife to cut a groove down the middle of the form in both places to better accommodate the bone ends on these fins *(figures 5-7 and 5-8)*. Check the fit of the form in the skin and make sure that the fins will set down in these grooves *(figure 5-9)*. If any additional cutting is necessary, do it now. Some cutting may be necessary at the vent fins indi-

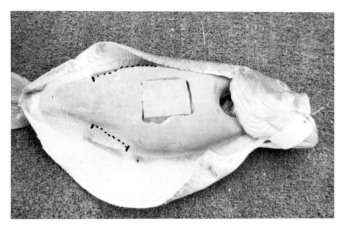

5-6

5-7

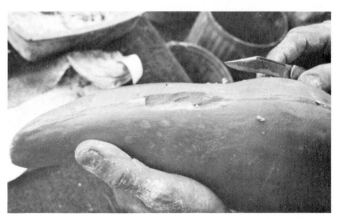

5-8

cated by the dotted line in figure 5-9. This will assure a good fit and keep the fins from bulging out.

STEP 4

Smear mache at the base of all fins *(figure 5-10)*. This will fill the grooves and gives the fins a smooth, firm fit.

STEP 5

Coat a wad of excelsior with mache and press this into the head cavity *(figure 5-11)*. Force it in to fill all of the

void spaces, checking with your hand on the other side for any soft spots. Figure 5-12 shows how this should appear when it has been packed in well.

STEP 6

Dab some mache on the rest of the exposed bones *(figure 5-13)* and fill the throat with the same excelsior, mache compound that was used for the head cavity *(figure 5-14)*.

5-9

5-12

5-10

5-13

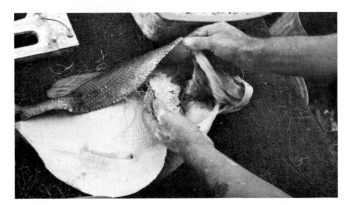

5-11

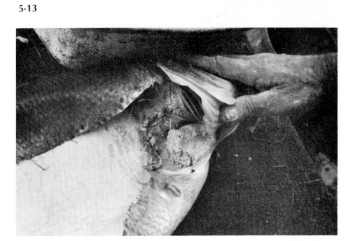

5-14

STEP 7

Check the fit of the form in the skin again and make all final adjustments that will be necessary before stapling *(figure 5-15)*. Also add some mache at the tail section now.

STEP 8

Put the first staple at the shoulder, pulling the skin down tight *(figure 5-16)*. Do this about halfway down the top edge, then pull the skin up tight and tack along the bottom edge *(figure 5-17)*. With a little practice, the stapling should take only a few minutes.

Pinch the skin together near the tail and make sure the form is fitting properly *(figure 5-18)*. Continue stapling down the top and then finish up on the bottom edge, making sure that all of the slack is taken up before the staples are put in *(figure 5-19)*. If you don't have a staple gun, the job may be done by pushing in straight pins.

STEP 9

Using mache, fill the gap where the form joins the head section *(figure 5-20)*. Fill it completely and smooth it out. All that is left now in the mounting process is to wash it off, fill the eyes with mache, and card the fins *(figure 5-21)*. For a detailed explanation on carding the fins, refer to the "Hollow Mount Method." The fish is now ready for drying.

5-17

5-15

5-18

5-16

5-19

5-20

5-21

HAND CARVED STYROFOAM BODIES

In the previous chapter we showed you a method of mounting, using factory forms for the fish. Styrofoam is usually easy to find locally and many people prefer to custom carve their forms. This is a common method, and with a little practice, it is easy to become fast and accurate.

STEP 1

With the skinned out meat, take a piece of solder and bend it around the meat to give you some idea of the curve that will be needed on the block *(figure 6-1)*. Keep the meat handy to check the carving by.

STEP 2

Lay the meat on an appropriate size piece of foam and use a marker to outline the body *(figure 6-2)*.

Saw along the outline with a hand saw or keyhole saw. A band saw works very well also if you have one *(figures 6-3 and 6-4)*.

STEP 3

Draw the curve that you want on the edge of the block. Be sure that this curve corresponds to the turn of the fish and the side that was skinned out *(figure 6-5)*. Cut this curve into the foam *(figure 6-6)*.

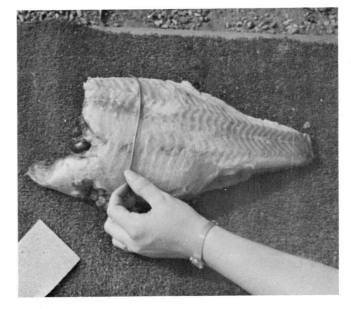

6-1

6-2

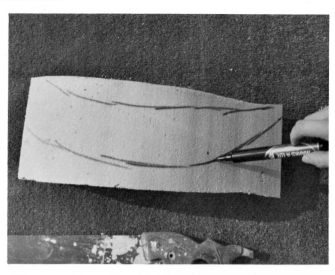

6-5

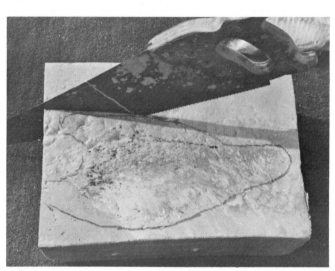

6-3

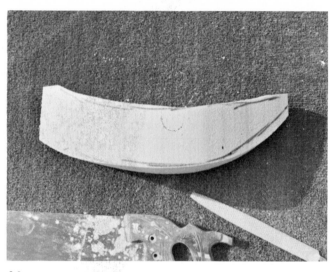

6-6

6-4

STEP 4

With a sharp knife, shave the edges and begin tapering them like the fish body *(figure 6-7)*. Next, using coarse sandpaper, begin smoothing the form and shaping it into contour *(figure 6-8)*. Check various points on the foam with the soldering wire and compare these measurements in the same places on the meat *(figure 6-9)*. It is a good idea to check the girth at the shoulder, the belly and tail section using this method.

Continue sanding and shaping the body. A sanding disc with open coat works well on the styrofoam.

6-7

6-8

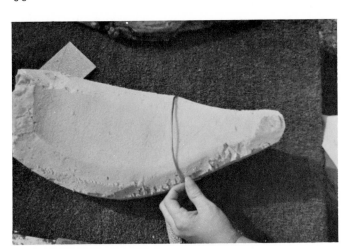

6-9

STEP 5

With the form completed *(figure 6-10)* you are now ready to start the mounting process. Refer to Chapter 5 which explains in detail the steps for mounting with foam bodies.

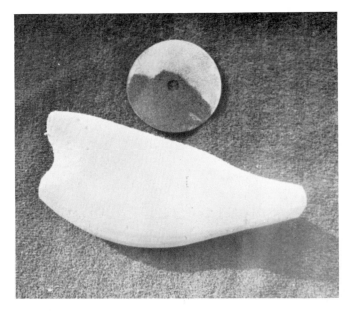

6-10

PRECISION FOAM CARVING FOR THIN SKIN FISH SUCH AS TROUT

Because of the availability of various inexpensive foams, and the ease with which it works, the foam carving method is quiet popular with many taxidermists. Unlike working with heavily scaled fish, trout present a very different problem. There is some room for error when making a foam body for a bass mount, but this is not so with trout and other thin skinned fish. Every detail must be right or the mount will simply be unacceptable. A lot of freehand and guesswork can be used on bass, but everything must be accurate on the trout.

STEP 1

Lay the trout on a piece of stiff brown paper, giving yourself enough room to trace around the fish. Make the curve on the fish that you want now *(figure 7-1)* either upward or downward and with a wax crayon, outline the fish on the paper. Be very accurate when you trace under the throat and draw a mark straight out from the front of the throat at the point where the tip of the foam should come *(figures 7-2 and 7-3)*. Make a mark at the top of the head also, at the point where the top of the foam should come *(figure 7-4)*. It should be where the scales end and the smooth part of the head begins.

Remove the fish from the paper now and touch up the curved sections making nice, smooth, flowing lines like that of the fish *(figure 7-5)*.

7-1

7-2

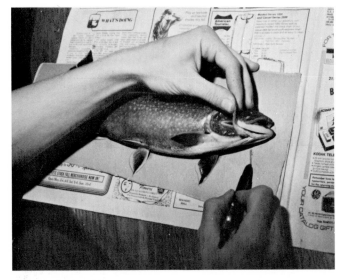

7-3

7-4

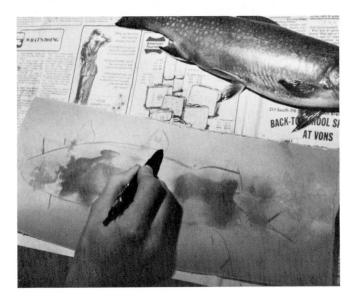

7-5

STEP 2

With a cloth tape measure, take four accurate measurements from the fish itself *(figure 7-6)*: 1. at the small part of the tail, 2. at the anus, 3. just in front of the dorsal fin, and 4. right behind the gills. Mark these measurements on the paper in their proper places. You will need to take one more measurement with a pair of calipers to get the thickness of the fish *(figure 7-7)*. Mark the thickness and the point at which the measurement was taken on the paper. To get the thickness, measure between the points of the calipers *(figure 7-8)*.

7-6

7-7

7-8

STEP 3

Cut the pattern out *(figure 7-9)* and outline this on a block of styrofoam *(figure 7-10)*.

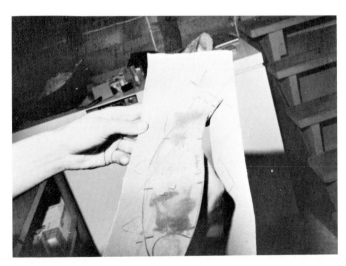

7-9

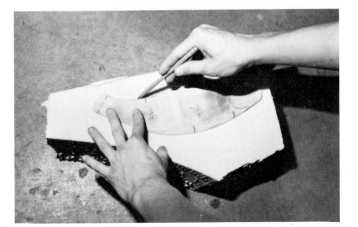

7-10

STEP 4

With a small keyhole saw, begin cutting the foam *(figure 7-11)*. Short easy strokes are best for this kind of cutting. When you have cut the form completely out, shape up the rough sides with a Surfoam scraper *(figure 7-12)*. Sandpaper or files can also be used to do this.

7-11

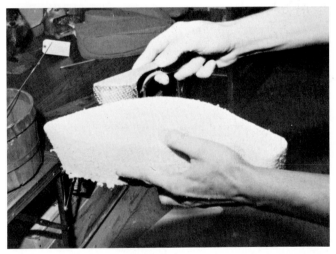

7-12

7-13

STEP 5

Using the measurements that were taken from the calipers, layout the thickness and the outward curve on the form *(figure 7-13)*. Working from the basic measurements that you have, a little free hand and imagination can be used here to draw in the curve that you want *(figure 7-14)*.

STEP 6

Hold the foam block securely and saw in a smooth straight manner. Start at the head section and follow your outline to the tail on both sides, being careful not to break the form at the tail *(figures 7-15 and 7-16)*. Smooth the sides with the scraper again and take off the edges with a thin blade knife *(figure 7-17)*. Continue with the knife as the body begins to take shape and use light strokes to remove the foam, being careful not to dig in too deep and make gaps.

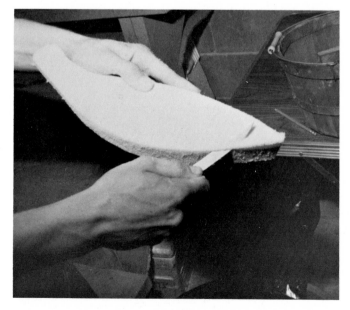

7-16

7-14

STEP 7

As the form nears completion, use your scraper, checking your measurements from time to time, making sure that you stay within those sizes. The overall body can be from ½ inch to ¾ inch larger than the actual body. This will give the fish a fuller look.

Use a sanding block and continue shaping *(figure 7-18)*. Another piece of foam can also be used to shape the body. Just rub it against the form and it will smooth like sandpaper. Check your measurements at least once more before finishing this step.

7-15

7-17

STEP 8

Mark the top of the head section and the lower throat in the place that is marked on your pattern. These are critical points and must be accurate *(figure 7-19)*. Freehand this curve on the form and carefully saw it out of the body *(figure 7-20)*. Clean out this area with a sharp knife *(figure 7-21)* and taper the edges of this cut to allow the bone section to sit down into the form *(figure 7-22)*. Smooth this throat area with sandpaper.

Make a final check of your measurements and lightly sand any areas that are not smooth or in contour.

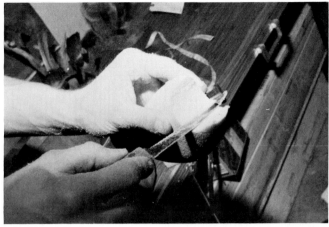

7-21

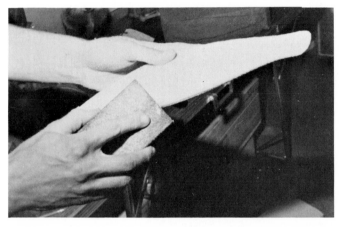

7-18

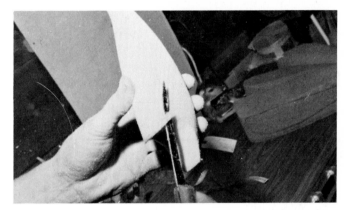

7-22

STEP 9

To attach the mounting block, cut a square section the size of the piece of wood you are using out of the back of the form with a putty knife *(figure 7-23)*. Glue the block of wood in with glue that works on styrofoam and make a snug fit that is level with the foam body *(figure 7-24)*.

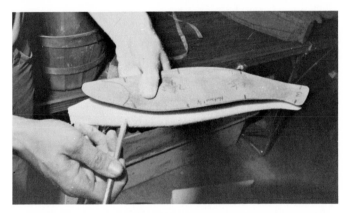

7-19

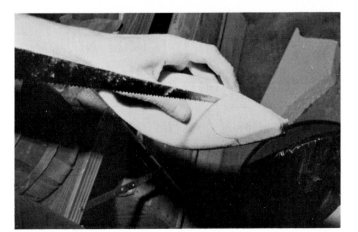

7-20

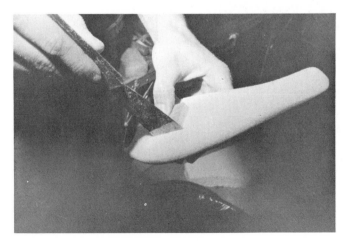

7-23

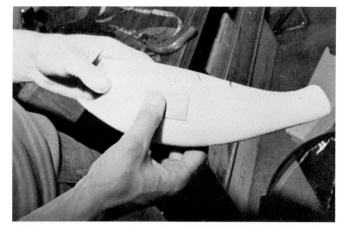

7-24

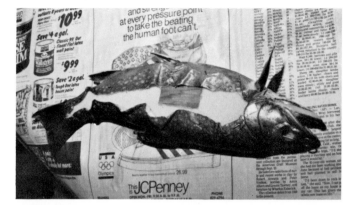

7-26

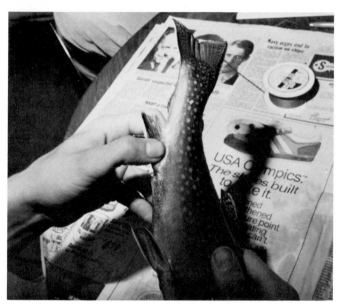

7-27

FOR CONVENTIONAL MOUNTING

STEP 1

Mix a handful of borax for each gallon of water and let the skin soak in this solution overnight. You should be ready to put the form into the skin the next day.

STEP 2

When you begin adjusting the skin to fit the form, further sanding is occasionally necessary but the form usually fits *(figure 7-25)*. Using straight pins, start fitting and pinning all of the skin onto the back of the form. Check the front (show) side and adjust the skin until it fits snugly without any wrinkles or flaws *(figure 7-26)*. Gently press the bone structure into the foam and take up the slack at the tail *(figure 7-27)*.

STEP 3

When you have fitted the skin satisfactorily, start sewing the skin back together at the tail and removing the pins *(figure 7-28)*. Don't pull the skin too hard or you may tear out the stitches. Keep checking the front to make sure the skin well as you stitch up the back.

STEP 4

Pin the gills down and press the bone into the foam for a tight fit *(figure 7-29)*. To adjust the head insert a pin or sharp wire into the nostril and move the head to the desired position *(figure 7-30)*.

FOR FREEZE DRIED TREATMENT ONLY

Take the skinned trout and wash it in clean water. Then run it through the #1 freeze dry bath for one minute. Move it to the #2 freeze dry bath and leave it for one minute and after this run it through #3 freeze dry bath for **two** minutes.

7-25

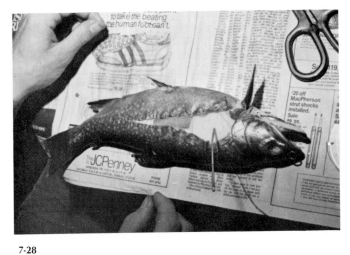

7-28

7-29

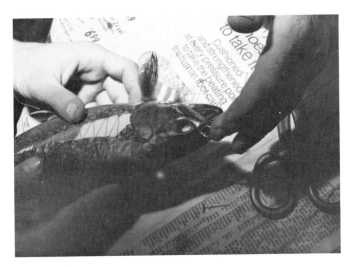

7-30

FOR FREEZE DRY FISH ONLY

Draw some inject-a-fill into a hypodermic needle and inject it into the meaty section of the head. Use your fingers to spread the bulge out *(figure 7-31)*. Inject into the cheek area of the trout and once again smooth it out *(figure 7-32)*. Card all of the fins and the fish is now ready for drying the conventional or freeze dry method *(figure 7-33)*.

7-31

7-32

7-33

FREEZE DRY MOUNTING

As in all trades, new methods come along for improvement of the art. In the field of taxidermy, one of the latest innovations is the freeze dry method.

Freeze dry, or Lyophilization is a method of preserving specimen by pulling a vacuum and keeping the specimen frozen until all of the moisture has been removed. It is not my intention to explain exactly how this system works, but basically, what happens is that the machines cause the moisture to evaporate out of the specimen as a gas. Research for this system is not new. In the year 1813, William Hyde Wallaston introduced the principle to the Royal Society in London. He called the method "Sublimation."

The practical application of the system was not tested until Altman, in Leipzig, experimented with it at the turn of the century, but little research was done until Dr. H. T. Meryman of the Naval Medical Research Institute began to work with it, publishing his findings in 1960. After this, Dr. Roland Hower of the Smithsonian Institute began experimental work with a practical unit. He tried many specimen and developed techniques that could be applied to taxidermy.

I had seen the freeze dry units at the National Taxidermist Conventions, read the literature, and was curious. The thoughts of using one of these machines had run through my mind on many occasions, but I did not have sufficient information for a final decision until I visited The North Star Freeze Dry Company, P. O. Box 439, Pequot Lakes, Minn. 56472. At this plant I met the owner, Mr. Roger Saatzer and the sales and marketing man, Jerry

Dobbs. Their modern plant was turning out freeze dry machines in various sizes for different needs. The success of this company indicates that the taxidermy trade is beginning to learn what an aid and tool these machines are for the speed and efficiency they provide.

I had many unanswered questions about the system and how it worked. After spending two days with these folks, I was convinced that I had to have one of those "strange looking monsters," which performed these seemingly miraculous feats.

The thought of what was really going on in the chamber while the specimen was being frozen and dried, kept bothering me. How could the smell be removed? Was it some type of tanning, or did it replace the tanning process? Would it last indefinitely? Would the bugs get into it later? What happens to the oil in fat and oily fish? How much faster is it than conventional methods? I also wondered how it compared with the conventional methods in speed and the thought of it even replacing the taxidermist crossed my mind. Cost and practicality were also factors that had to be considered.

Roger and Jerry invited me to go with them and visit a man who had done much research and development on the process and had a successful taxidermy business based on this method.

We visited with Mr. Vic Birontas, one of the original designers of the system and an excellent taxidermist even before he had a machine.

In a short time, many of the questions that I had in my head were being answered for me. Vic began demonstrating his method with a crappie and worked through several other species. I watched the time it took for preparation, and began to mentally compare this to the time that I would normally use, bringing different fish off the line using conventional taxidermy. On small fish, up to the size of a crappie, I estimated my preparation time to be cut in half, and if I ran a large group together, it could be even less.

In talking to Vic, he explained that when a fish weighed more than 31 pounds, and was 21 inches or longer, he used a foam body and skinned the fish, leaving the meat in the head. This method makes the drying process very fast and keeps the heads of fish like trout from drying down which eliminates build up work. The oil problem can be solved with the larger fish by the conventional methods of scraping and using solvents. Smaller fish are injected with an antioxidant.

According to some specialist, some fish have their own antioxidants in the skin, which when freeze dried, lock up the oils and no "bleeding" will occur. Much research needs to be done in this area and we are, at the present time, working with numerous oily salt water fish to see what methods work best.

With a sufficient number of fish that lend themselves to the freeze dry method, and with the addition of various other animals and items, a freeze dry machine can be a very worthwhile tool. The machine can be used to do other taxidermist freeze dry articles on a lease or commission basis when you have extra space in the machine that is not being utilized.

A freeze dry technician who is not a quality taxidermist cannot expect to turn out quality work, but skill in the taxidermy trade can make you a skilled freeze dry taxidermist if you are interested enough to learn.

MOUNTING A CRAPPIE THE FREEZE DRY METHOD

Unlike the conventional methods I have discussed in this book, other than fiberglass reproductions, in this method, the fish is not skinned and only the eyes are removed. You must also have a freeze dry machine or at least have one available for your use, and though this alone may keep you from experimenting with this method, I think it is well worth your time to examine all possibilities.

In preparing the fish for freeze drying, various chemical baths are needed, and these products can be purchased from the North Star Company. Three separate baths are needed; bath #1 contains endolan-U, a strong insect and rodent proofing chemical; bath #2 is a type of acid which locks the first solution into the skin; bath #3 cleans up the excess of #1 and #2, and also adds some rodent proofing. You will also need a solution called Injectafil which is an aqueous plastic designed for restoring muscle areas which have a tendency to dry down.

STEP 1

Add two ounces of bath #1 per gallon of water. This bath has a sulphonamide system incorporating a built in shampoo, and is PH balanced. It also has a color indicator which will turn the bath from blue to grey when it becomes weak and worn out. Add one ounce of bath #2 to each gallon of water, and bath #3 comes ready to use. We usually mix the baths in three separate two and one half gallon buckets (figure 8-1). Wash the fish off in clean water before the baths.

STEP 2

With a scalpel or a sharp knife, remove the eyes. Hold the fish by the eye sockets and swish the fish gently in the first bath for about one minute. Make sure that the fish is completely submerged in the solution, even the part that you are holding. Follow the same procedure in bath #2 with the fish, and then move to bath #3 where you should drop the entire fish in the solution and leave it for two minutes (figure 8-2).

8-1

STEP 3

Lay the fish on some newspaper and dry it off with a paper towel *(figure 8-3)*. Pour some Injectafil into a small bowl and draw it into a hypodermic needle. Inject this into the head cavity and cheek areas of the fish *(figure 8-4)*. Smooth any areas that may bulge out, with your fingers *(figure 8-5)*.

8-4

8-2

8-5

8-3

STEP 4

Card the fins using stiff board and pre-cut screen wire *(figure 8-6)*. This is a slight variation on the usual method which is explained in detail in Chapter 1.

STEP 5

When the fish is completely carded, it is ready for positioning. Push pins through the cardboard into the board which the fish is lying on, to position the fins *(figure 8-7)*. You can also use small wedges of styrofoam to prop the fins up. To position the spiny dorsal, raise it up and put a pin at the first ray, as shown by the arrow in Figure 8-8. Notice that the board on which the fish is lying has been covered with wax paper. This will help it come off the board after it has been frozen. The pins are driven into the board and the tail can be raised to the proper height for the curve *(figure 8-8)*.

STEP 6

The fish is now ready to be placed in any kind of freezer. Vic Birontas had a walk-in freezer, and freeze dry combination.

STEP 7

After overnight freezing, remove the fish and drill three half-inch holes in the back of the fish *(figure 8-9)*. This will speed up the drying time. It is then placed in a freeze dry machine and left for about two weeks.

Most operators say that when seventy percent of the moisture is removed, it is finished. Others will remove the fish when they know it is not loosing any more weight. All specimen should be weighed before they are placed in the freeze dry machine, that way you will know when "sublimation" is finished. The cut-a-way shows what the inside of the fish looks like when it is dried *(figure 8-10)*.

Paint the fish in the usual manner.

8-6

8-7

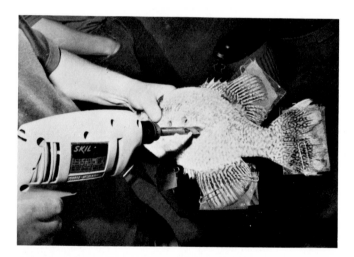

8-9

8-8

8-10

Freeze Dry Method With Foam Carved Bodies

Using this method, larger fish can be mounted with conventional foam bodies, but the meat can be left in the head. This is an advantage because the heads of some fish, especially trout, will shrink down in the drying process unless a lot of care is taken to remove all of the meat.

Use the methods illustrated in Chapter Seven to carve the foam bodies. The freeze drying will leave the head nice and smooth with no filling required. This is a very fast method for trout.

Vic Birontas and his freezer, freeze dry unit combination.

BEHIND THE SCENES OF THE NORTH STAR FREEZE DRY COMPANY

Jerry Dobbs and the plant manager are continuing to research and improve the freeze dry methods.

The welding of the tanks must be done with extreme skill to eliminate any leaks.

Inspections are a continuing process as the equipment is assembled.

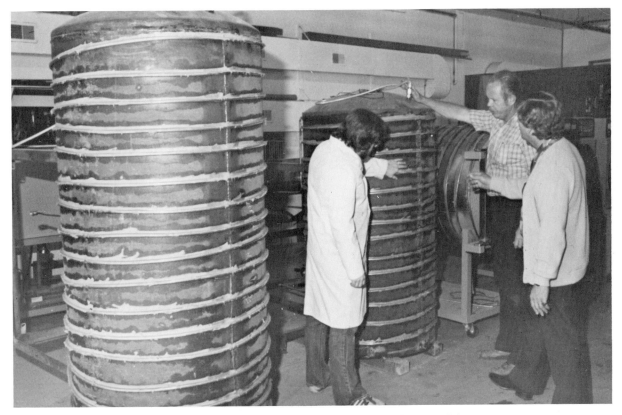

Each tank must be lined in such a way to give maximum efficiency.

New models for various needs are continuously being brought off the line.

All machines are pre-tested at the factory to insure good service.

Roger Saatzer and wife Fran answer numerous requests for information on uses of this revolutionary new concept.

In addition to freeze dry machines, a line of tumblers were added to speed the taxidermist's work.

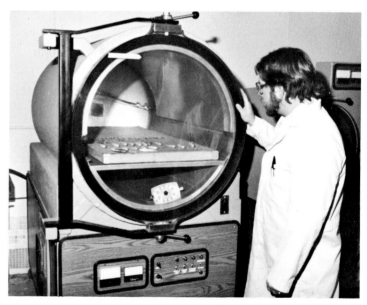

New and innovative ways to use the machines are tried.

FREEZE DRY
TAXIDERMY
SHOWCASE

ALL OF THE SUBJECTS IN THESE PHOTOS ARE THE WORK OF VIC BIRONTAS OF NISSWA, MINNESOTA.

Vic Birontas in his showroom in Nisswa, Minnesota.

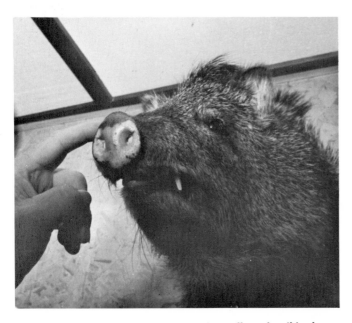

Notice the lack of shrinkage and excellent detail in the boar's head.

Vic with a wide variety of subjects that he uses in his operation.

Combination fish display — foam bodies and freeze dried.

Snakes are one item that most taxidermist turn down, but they are a snap with the freeze dry machine. They maintain all of their muscle characteristics and can be posed in any position.

The attitude of any type of bird can be varied with greater ease using this method than with any other.

A habitat setting would enhance any den.

Small fish in an underwater scene makes a nice table piece.

This award winning badger has nice facial details and overall appearance.

Items inside the freeze dry machine

The lake trout has always plagued the taxidermist because of the oil problem. This one was treated with the antioxidant and has held up well.

Froggy goes a courting — these are excellent subjects.

A mother and kitten bobcat.

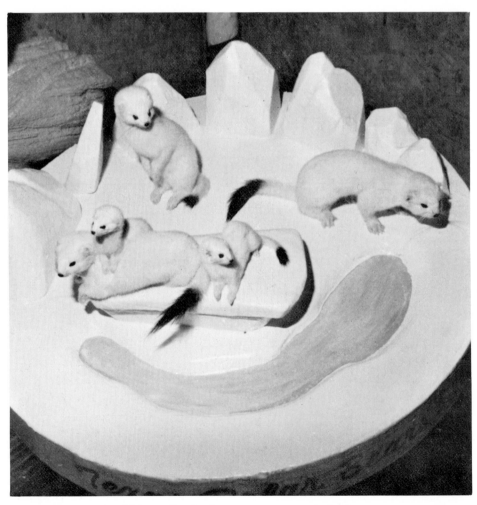

This small animal group was very easy to do.

The otter looks as though he is ready to slip off the rock and into the water.

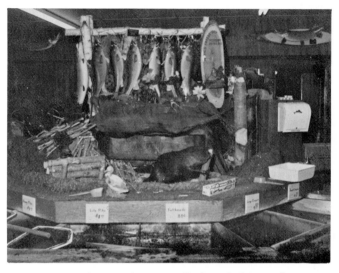

A sporting goods store's display of Vic's work.

Nothing excites fishermen more than a stringer mount of largemouth bass.

A nice string of large smallmouth.

A taxidermist's skill, along with a freeze dry machine, can give results like this with birds.

Let's not forget about the crappie fisherman; anyone would like to carry a stringer like that home.

Walleyes galore — what a beautiful setting

These species look as if they will retreat at any moment.

The northern pike is one of the "bread and butter" fish of the north.

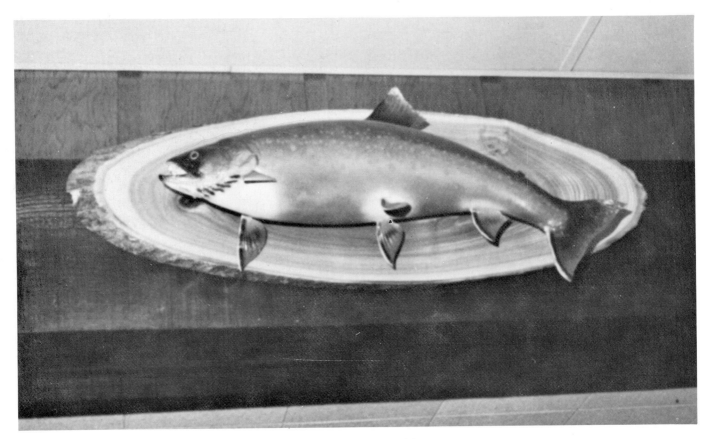

The Char makes a nice subject.

Artic greyling can be completely done in the machine. The grace and curves are truly beautiful.

The bear cub has nice detail, especially around the nose and face.

Note the quality of the face of this deer mount.

This mount looks so much alive — it could fool anyone.

PREPARING REPRODUCTION FISH

FIBERGLASS VS. SKIN MOUNTS

Many new and wonderful products are springing onto the market in ever increasing numbers, but the one that concerns taxidermists, and probably has caused a greater re-evaluation of the art, is fiberglass. After years of using and molding with fiberglass, I have found that for some jobs it can't be beat, and for others the conventional method is best. Both methods are described in this book.

There is no question that all species of fish can be reproduced in fiberglass, and some of the largest shops do only fiberglass work. However, not all fish are as easy to do in fiberglass as skin mounts. For example, we mount all of our customers' bass with skin mounts for two reasons: (1) it is more economical in time and material; and (2) the lag time is less.

When mounting salt water fish some are so full of oil that the best degreasing methods will not produce a satisfactory job. The tarpon is a good example. We have mounted many under 36 inches that were not much trouble. For the big ones, it seems like the oil will never stop oozing. I have repaired many old skin mounts that had this oil problem and no one to my knowledge, has solved it as yet. Shrinkage can be another problem with skin mounts and the necessary filler can at times blot out a lot of detail. Note the shrinkage in the head section of the brown trout *(figure 9-1)*.

One opinion voice against reproductions is, "This isn't my real fish." In many a case, such as shark, it must be a reproduction or your customer cannot have a mount. (I have mounted sharks with skins, and they were entirely unsatisfactory.) The opposite opinion would be, "In taxidermy our job is to restore to life-like appearance, using any medium that is at our disposal, because the finished product is the real test of craftsmanship." When someone brings in a deer head, the skull is thrown away and replaced with a modern urethane form, artificial eyes, plastic earliners, painted nose, and often even plastic teeth. So where do you draw the line?

Regardless of personal preference, the fiberglass fish has opened a new market for taxidermists — the interior decorator, restaurant business, and other commercial customers. Heretofore, I had no products for this market except an occasional unclaimed specimen. Now, I sell many catfish, red snapper, and other species which add to the atmosphere of a restaurant. Frequently decorators want fiberglass reproductions of large marine specimens.

After much experimenting, I have found that for our shop some specimens are best reproduced in fiberglass while skin mounts are preferred for others. This varies depending on what you feel more comfortable using.

FRESH WATER SPECIES

Bass — skin mounts preferred. Glass for commercial sales.

Bream, crappie, all panfish — skin mounts preferred.

Northern pike, muskies, walleyes — skin mounts.

Rainbows and smaller trout — either way is satisfactory.

Coho salmon, lake trout — smaller specimens skin mounted, larger specimens are better in fiberglass due to oil.

Catfish — reproduce.

SALT WATER SPECIES

Sailfish, mackerel, bonito, wahoo, shark, ray, eel, marlin, tuna, etc. — reproduce in glass or forget it.

Red snapper, redfish, rockfish, ling, sheepshead, barracuda, speckled trout, most scale-type fish — skin mounts.

Tarpon — reproduce, especially on larger sizes.

9-1

The fish blanks made in Archie Phillips' Taxidermy Studio are filled with urethane foam, with a surface of white gel coat backed with polyester resin and fiberglass matt. Fiberglass fins are also supplied. Our catalog lists hundreds of standard models, and custom poses are available.

Besides not having to worry about the problems that come with painting skin mounts, reproduction mounts have other advantages. One good feature of the reproduction model is being able to attach the fish hangers with pop rivets. Screws can be inserted into the imbedded wood block making this convenient and faster than other methods of mounting. Foam filling gives the fish a more ''real'' feel and makes the mouth easier to shape. Also the inert composition of fiberglass means a longer lasting mount without the repairs that are sometimes necessary on skin mounts. Remember, it is painting the reproduction to truly reflect the spirit of the original that really counts.

The following steps may seem time consuming and expensive; but the volume of increased business generated should soon prove this method is a worthwhile investment.

STEP 1

Fiberglass fish blanks come with a small flashing that extends from the center line which must be trimmed away. Use a knife or heavy shears to do this. Once the excess has been removed, an adjustable speed Dremel moto-tool with a coarse sanding drum attachment is an ideal tool for smoothing this flashing down to the mold line, but be careful not to grind into the fin or body detail *(figure 9-2)*. Use a smooth, easy stroke, taking off a little at a time. A file can also be used for this, but it will take longer.

9-2

STEP 2

Use a cone shaped bit to clean out tight areas around the base of the fins *(figure 9-3)*. Carbide steel bits work best since they are most durable.

For further finishing around the fins use a small round file and a small flat one *(figure 9-4)*.

9-5

9-3

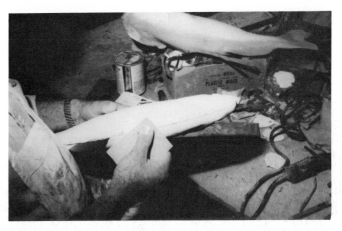

9-6

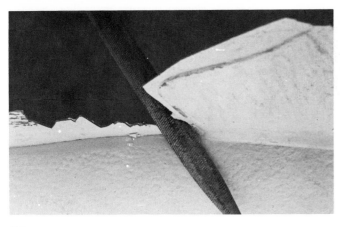

9-4

STEP 3

If you have one available, an air grinder is the best tool for cleaning out the mouth. The moto-tool will do, but it will take a little longer. Don't cut below the lip line of the fish and always work with the tool slanting to the inside. A cone bit is good for hard to get areas and finishing *(figure 9-5)*.

STEP 4

Sand the flashing with 80 grit sandpaper to knock off any small burrs *(figure 9-6)*.

STEP 5

To smooth out the seam that will be left by the flashing, use fish putty or bondo — the same kind you get at automotive parts stores. Cheaper fillers tend to gum up on the sandpaper.

Mix the filler according to the directions that come with it. It has a resin base and looks much like putty. If a red hardener is used, mix it to a dusty rose color. Too much hardener will make the putty brittle and not enough will diminish its hardening power. This compound usually sets up in about three minutes, allow longer in cold weather, so don't mix too much at one time.

Spread the bondo down the seam using a flexible, metal spatula. Apply down the entire length of the fish, top and bottom and fill any other rough area that may need work also *(figure 9-7)*. Press it hard, smoothing the edges to the fiberglass *(figure 9-8)*.

STEP 6

Allow at least twenty minutes before sanding this. Use 80 grit sandpaper first and sand in contour with the fish, feathering out the edge so that it blends well. Use a fine sandpaper, #150 or #200 to finish this *(figure 9-9)*.

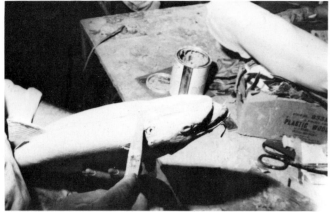

9-7

9-8

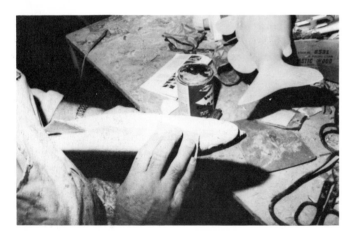

9-9

9-10

9-11

STEP 8

Use the moto-tool to clean out an area large enough for the eye that you will be using *(figure 9-12)*.

Insert the eye with a small amount of bondo *(figure 9-13)*, and when it sets, use a knife to cut away the excess

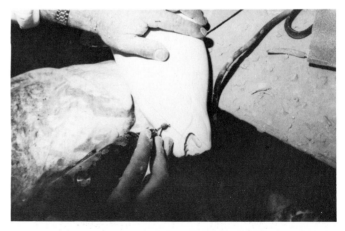

9-12

STEP 7

Use scissors to cut out the fins that have to be attached *(figure 9-10)*. Cut about one eighth inch to the outside of the outline and smooth this extra down to the margin with the moto-tool *(figure 9-11)*. Taper the back edges of the fins to make them thinner and more natural looking.

bondo. Sand into contour not letting the sandpaper touch the eye. Clean the eye with laquer thinner.

9-13

STEP 9

The fins that we use have a key put into them for strength. Drill a hole to receive the fin for a neat, flush fit *(figure 9-14)*. On the pectoral fin, it is not always necessary to use the key which can be ground off and the fin fitted into a filed groove. Insert the fin and fill the joint with bondo *(figure 9-15)*.

A small round file can be used to shape the bondo *(figure 9-16)*. Use sandpaper to smooth it out. Finish these fins the same way the seams on the back and bottom were finished.

Mount the vent fins the same way, and check the specimen you are reproducing or a photograph of that specie to determine the correct angle *(figure 9-17)*. Be careful to avoid placing the back ventricle fin so that it presses against the panel *(figure 9-18)*. Finish the joints with bondo and sand to the contour of the fish *(figure 9-19)*.

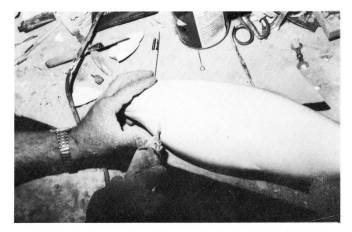

9-14

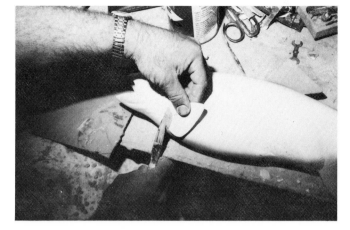

9-15

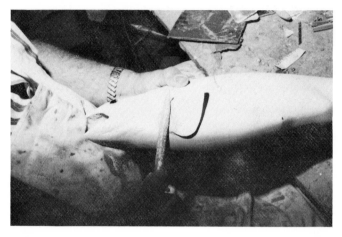

9-16

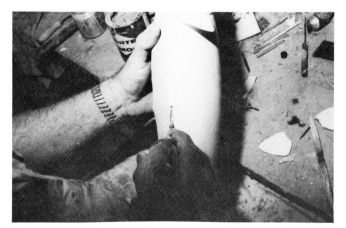

9-17

9-18

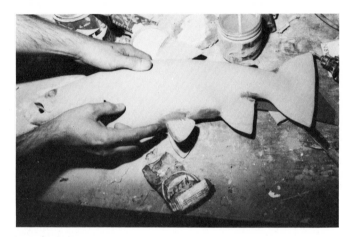

9-19

STEP 10

Apply automotive prime with an airbrush *(figure 9-20).* Spray it on lightly to avoid blotting out any scale texture.

When the primer is dry, check the fish thoroughly for any small scratches or pin-holes that need filling. Automotive pin-hole-filler or glazing putty works well for

this, but it is only for the small jobs. If much filling is needed, go back to the resin putty. Let the glazing putty dry for ten minutes before sanding. Sand with #220 sandpaper, spot prime these areas, and sand lightly again *(figure 9-21).*

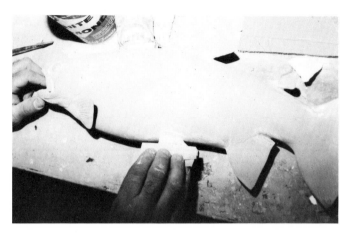

9-21

STEP 11

Mix enough bondo to spread inside the mouth, top and bottom *(figure 9-22).* Apply with a putty knife and smooth it out with a brush dipped in acetone. Do this quickly and it will save you a lot of sanding later. Fill the mouth with enough bondo to make it look natural.

Acetone, available at chemical supply companies, is also good for cleaning tools and brushes. It evaporates quickly and is best stored in Tupperware plastic containers. Do not store in other plastic containers, because the acetone will eat through many of them.

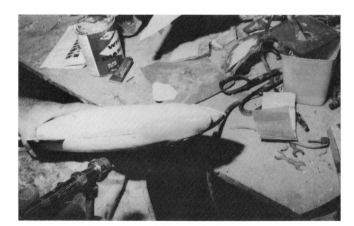

9-20

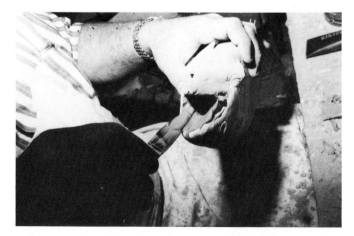

9-22

REPRODUCING FISH TEETH

I have found that bondo is also an excellent compound for reproducing teeth on such fish as barracuda, trout, and shark, when using fiberglass blanks. There is a simple procedure for this and with practice, any shape tooth can be made.

Figure 9-23 illustrates this procedure on trout. Using a round toothpick, pull a drop of bondo up from the base of the lip line to form the tooth. Turn the fish over and do this on the other jaw also.

The barracuda has a flat sawtooth and these teeth are also easy to make. Take a small amount of the bondo or plastic body filler on the end of a round toothpick, touch it to the lip line and form the tooth by pulling it up and back at a slight angle (figure 9-24). Make sure that the teeth are similar to the ones on the fish you are trying to reproduce. The barracuda has two rows of teeth. The inside row is done in the same manner (figure 9-25).

After the teeth have been made on fiberglass blanks, the inside of the mouth should be painted with gel coating, Elmers Glue, or sanding sealer (figure 9-26). I use gel coating, which is a fiberglass resin pigment mixed with a catalyst. Fiberglass supply companies carry this. Painting the teeth with any of the above creates a good, more lifelike effect on the finished mount.

We usually use the original teeth on a shark mount although they can be made with bondo also.

To use real shark teeth, soak the jawbone, with teeth intact in solox. Next, wash them and let them dry thoroughly. Once they are bone dry, the back edge of the jawbone should be sanded or filed down until the base of the teeth is reached (figure 9-27).

The teeth will probably have to be shaped with your hands in order to fit the mouth properly. They seldom fit exactly right (figure 9-28).

The inside of the mouth should be sanded and smooth and ready to receive the teeth. Place the fitted teeth in the proper position and use bondo to hold them in place (figures 9-29 and 9-30). The mouth will probably need some additional sanding after the teeth have been fitted,

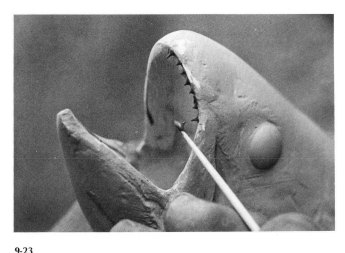

9-23

9-25

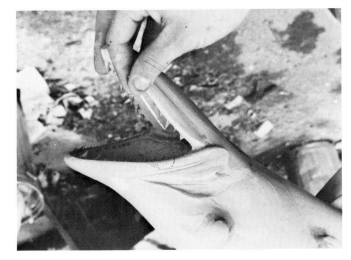

9-24

9-26

9-27

9-28

9-29

to smooth out the bondo *(figure 9-31)*. When you are satisfied, paint inside the mouth with gel coating.

To use real barracuda teeth on fiberglass mounts, the procedure will be much the same as it is for shark teeth. However, using barracuda teeth you will have to work with smaller fragments of the jawbone *(figures 9-32 and 9-33)*.

After the teeth have been made and the mouth is completed, go over the entire fish with #00 steel wool to prepare it for painting. Be sure to get into the curves and blow the dust off thoroughly.

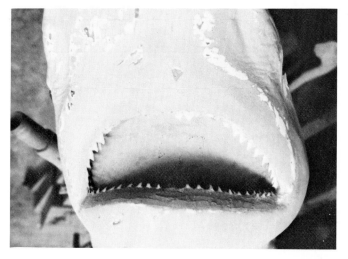

9-30

9-31

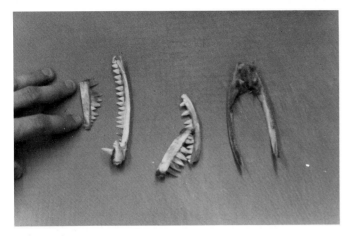

9-32

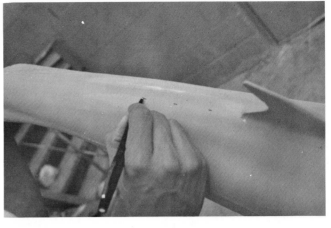

9-34

9-33

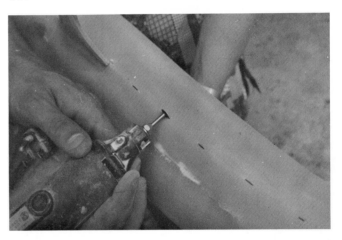

9-35

ATTACHING FINLETS TO FIBERGLASS BODIES

Some fish, such as bonito, wahoo, various tuna and various other saltwater fish have small finlets that run from the sub-dorsal and sub-anal fins back toward the tail. These have to be made and attached on the fiberglass body by the taxidermist. This is one of the few preparations necessary when doing a fiberglass mount and there is a simple procedure for this.

First, check the fish at hand and count the finlets, top and bottom, that it has.

Then use a felt tip pen and mark the places they will be on the fiberglass body, spacing them as on the original (figure 9-34). If you don't have the specimen, look for a picture in a book to go by. This is one of the many reasons it is to your advantage to start some type of reference file, collecting as many pictures of different species as possible.

Using a moto tool with a saw blade, cut one groove for each finlet (figure 9-35).

Now you will need some type of stiff paper to make the finlets and quick drying epoxy glue for attaching them.

"Fish" paper which is used in the electronics industry and is not hard to find, is excellent for the finlets although any stiff, thin paper, which is not waxy, can be used.

Cut a narrow strip of paper and, using a sharp pair of scissors, cut the wedge shapes as shown in figure 9-36. Notice the difference in the two shown.

Mix a small amount of epoxy according to the directions that come with it. Make sure it is mixed thoroughly. If it isn't, it won't dry properly and will mess up your painting.

Have all of the finlets that will be needed for the entire fish ready. Dip the front, or short end of the finlet into the epoxy and draw the dab or epoxy that you will pick up across the saw cut to fill it. Then insert the finlet into this groove and position it vertically (figure 9-37).

Continue all the way down the top or bottom, moving swiftly to finish one side before the epoxy hardens (figure 9-38).

Once the glue begins to harden, go back and check to make sure none of the finlets have sagged or gotten out of line. It is important that they are all uniform. Continue this process on the other side to complete the job. When the fish is sprayed with primer, you may notice some small cracks or pin holes that didn't get filled with the epoxy. If so, use pin hole filler, or a drip from the primer can to take care of these.

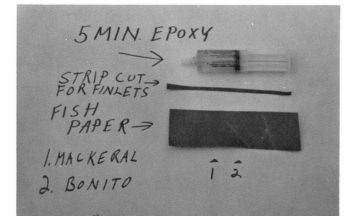

9-36

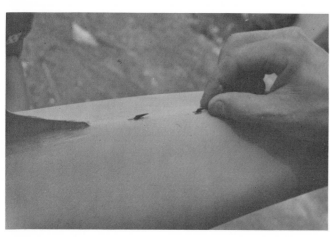

9-37

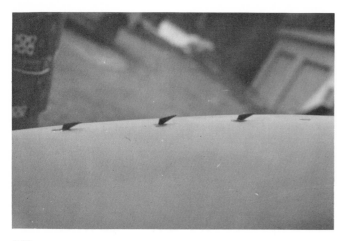

9-38

PREPARING A SAILFISH BLANK

STEP 1

Trim away all of the flashing from the blank using a saw, tin snips, rotary files or other methods *(figure 9-39)*. Follow the outline of the blank and cut all of the surplus away from the fins (figure 9-40).

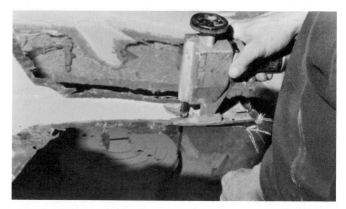

9-39

9-40

STEP 2

Dap out the fins with a moto tool or a grinder. Notice the curve in these sections and try to make this as smooth and as graceful as possible *(figure 9-41)*.

STEP 3

Cut away the fiberglass in the mouth now, but don't get too close to the edge on the first cut *(figure 9-42)*. Leave at least 1/8" which you can grind away later. In other words, leave some margin for error. Cut from the front into the corner of the mouth on top and bottom, then remove this section *(figure 9-43)*.

Finish taking the surplus out of the mouth with an air grinder or moto tool *(figure 9-44)*. Be careful near the edges and don't take off too much.

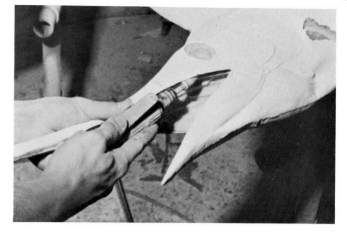

9-44

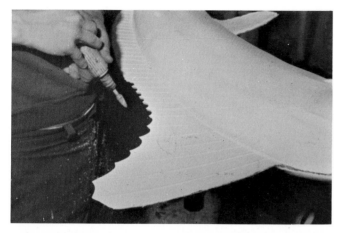

9-41

STEP 4

Remove all of the flashing from the pectoral fin and smooth it out. Place this fin on the body and mark the proper place to grind it for a tight fit *(figure 9-45)*. This fin should be tapered from top to bottom and toward the rear.

STEP 5

Be sure to remove all of the excess where the back of the fins meet the body *(figure 9-46)*.

STEP 6

Use a sander to smooth the rough edges of the fins and seams *(figure 9-47)*. Use about #80 grit sandpaper and sand lightly. It doesn't take much. I usually take the glaze off areas that are to receive bondo *(figure 9-48)*.

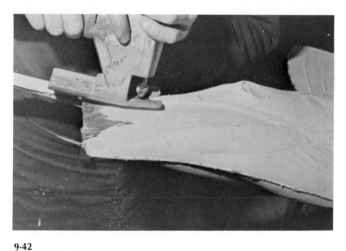

9-42

9-43

9-45

9-46

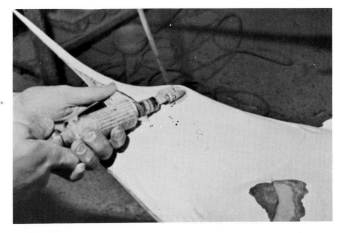

9-49

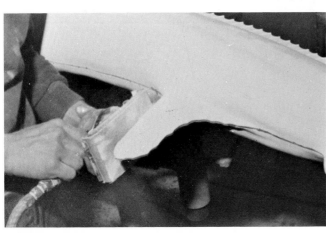

9-47

9-50

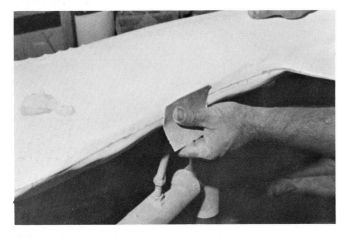

9-48

9-51

STEP 7

Grind out the eye socket to receive the eye. Also note the area that was ground out to receive the fin (figure 9-49).

Fill the eye socket with bondo and insert the eye, adjusting it to look natural (figure 9-50).

Use bondo to connect the fin to the body of the fish also. Smooth it out around the base of the fin and use any handy item to prop it up while the bondo sets (figure 9-51).

STEP 8

Fill the mouth, top and bottom, up to the edges, with bondo. Smooth it down firmly with a spatula. Notice that enough pressure is applied to the spatula to make it bend (figure 9-52), as it is brought forward from the back of the mouth. This gives the bottom of the jaw a slight curve and makes a nice finish.

STEP 9

After the seam has been sanded smooth, apply only as much bondo as is necessary to fill all voids and bad places along the seam *(figure 9-53)*. When this dries, sand it smooth and go over the seams with a coat of primer surfacer applied with an airgun. This will make any areas that need additional work stand out better.

Use lacquer putty (pin hole filler) on any of these areas that are rough or have small holes, and apply it with your finger *(figure 9-54)*. This smooths out better if you dip your finger in lacquer thinner from time to time. Apply the putty liberally, and leave it overnight before sanding, if it is put on thick. Thin layers can be sanded in about 30 minutes. Areas around the eyes and fins usually need some attention.

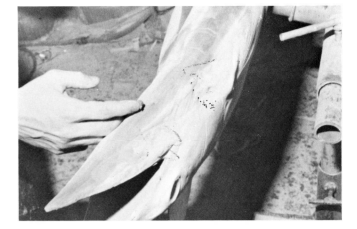

9-54

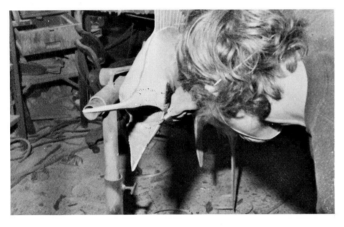

9-52

STEP 10

Sand the bondo inside the mouth smooth, then apply a thin coat of gel coating or sanding sealer on this area.

STEP 11

Paint the seams and other areas where filler was used again with primer, for one final check. If no further sanding is needed, spray the entire fish with primer surfacer *(figure 9-55)*. Fiberglass needs a good primer coating before the colors are applied.

With #220 grit sandpaper smooth out any imperfections and go over these areas with another light coat of primer *(figure 9-56)*.

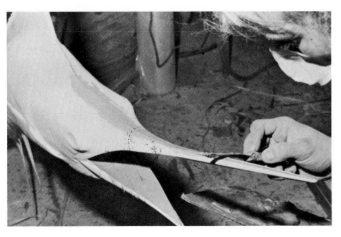

9-53

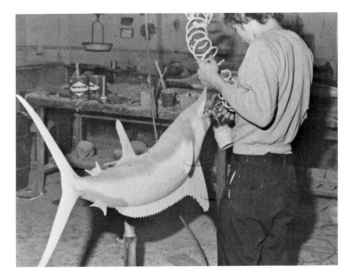

9-55

STEP 12

Mark the places where the vent fins will go. They should be directly under the pectoral fins *(figure 9-57)*. Use an air grinder or moto tool to make the slot.

Slip the two fins into the body pushing them into the foam inner core for a tight fit. Note the angle of these fins to the body *(figure 9-58)*. I usually remove the fins and fill the slots with bondo, then reinsert them. This makes a good permanent lock on the fins. Remove the surplus bondo and when it hardens, sand, fill and prime just as you did the other areas.

The fish is now ready to be painted.

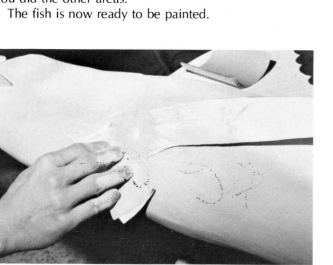

9-58

9-56

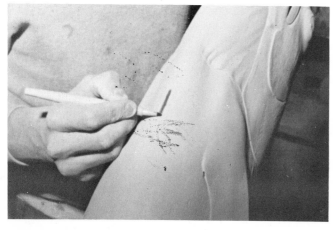

9-57

Many large saltwater fish that are impossible to mount with skins can now be done with fiberglass blanks. Shark mounts are now quite popular and these can be prepared several ways.

The series of photos below show the author preparing two different shark mounts.

Much modification must be done on this mount that was cut from a full mold.

Quarter mounts for sharks are now quite popular. The author is grinding the back edges to get them in contour with the wall.

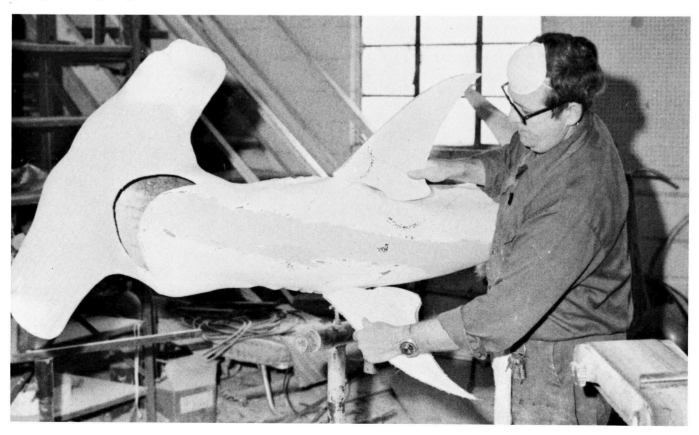

The author working up a model from a cast of a 400 lb. hammerhead shark.

PAINTING YOUR MOUNT

Practice in painting is extremely important. If you have never used an air brush, there is no substitute for sitting down with a paint gun and a piece of white cardboard and practicing to control colors, lines and spots *(figure 10-1)*. Outline the fish and practice painting the colors and patterns. It is also good to do this with a reproduction fish blank *(figure 10-2)*. Then drip the painted blank in a bath of lacquer thinner, brush it off, and paint it again. This changes the look of the fish considerably and will help train your eye to see how the fish looks before and after the final gloss coat is applied. Practice until you become so smooth with the air brush that your subconscious mind can almost take over. Like driving a car, air brush efficiency is best when you don't think about operating each control separately.

Take time to master color patterns using mental pictures of fish just out of the water; color photographs are also very useful. Examine fish from every angle, seeing where each color begins and ends. Learning to paint some fish makes it easier to paint others. For examples, when you learn to paint a smallmouth bass, the walleye pike and brown trout come naturally, the same follows with the bream and crappie. It is helpful to go to tournaments, where people will sometimes give you skins to study. Check books and magazines for color patterns, but be careful — the artist may have seen only one specimen. Try to compare at least three specimens before deciding on a basic pattern to work from.

Someone may tell you that they want a fish painted to look "natural." After taking over 4,000 slides of the largemouth bass, I have come to believe that there is no such thing as a "natural" colored fish. It is more important to find out what the customer feels is the natural color when he makes such a statement. A single species of fish can change colors with the weather and seasons, with muddy or clear water conditions, and with geographical location. Colors also change after fish have been frozen. It is a good idea to tag them with L-light, M-medium, or D-dark before freezing *(figure 10-3)*. True, it is the customer who must ultimately be pleased. I believe, however, that it is very important to have confidence in your own ability to interpret his fish based on your knowledge and ability. If you can communicate this to the customer, he will feel more confident about leaving his "prize" in your hands.

PREPARING YOUR MOUNT FOR PAINTING

STEP 1

Skin, stuff and shape the fish using one of the methods in this book. When the fish is dry, fill the seam in the back of the fish with plastic wood. Keep a jar of lacquer thinner and one of cellulose nitrate (thinned 50% with lacquer

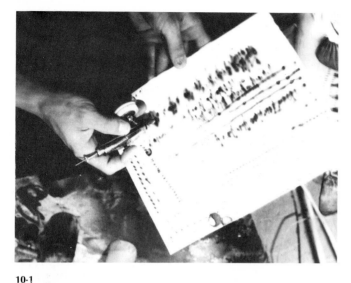

10-1

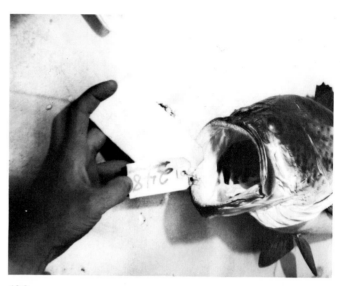

10-3

are good for cutting pressboard. Draw the fin outline, cut it out, and glue it onto the back of the fin with barge cement *(figures 10-7 and 10-8)*. Thin the barge cement with

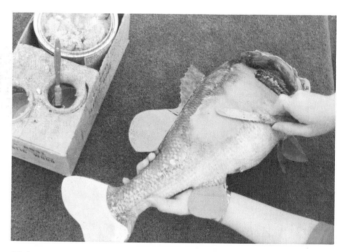

10-4

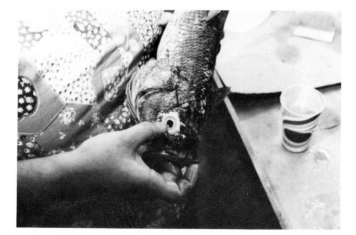

10-5

10-2

thinner) along with a can of plastic wood beside your work area *(figure 10-4)*. Smooth on the plastic wood with a small spatula, then paint cellulose nitrate over it with a brush. Let this dry at least 3 hours.

STEP 2

Fill the eye sockets with mache, and set in the eyes *(figure 10-5)*. Let dry; then dab plastic wood around the cracks *(figure 10-6)*. Smooth the plastic wood out with a finger dipped in cellulose nitrate. (Don't set the eye into wet plastic wood because it will eat the pigment off the back of the eye.)

STEP 3

Repair or replace any broken fins. Red pressboard seems to be best for this job. Genuine pressboard is resilent but will thump like a piece of metal. Poultry shears lacquer thinner or barge cement thinner so that it glides on. Don't let it get too thick, but be sure not to thin it until it loses its body and good holding power. Barge cement is available through shoe repair or supply stores and at my studio. Paint some of it on the back of the fin and some on the card, hole apart for 1 minute, then very carefully stick them together exactly right. Smooth out any air with your thumb, but do not try to slide the card around for a better fit. Trim card to contour of fin *(figure 10-9)*. Cut tail con-

tour to its natural shape *(figure 10-10)*. Taper lower edges of pressboard to make it stick down better . . . note wooden splint glued in place *(figure 10-11)*.

10-9

10-6

10-7

10-10

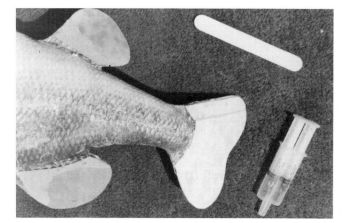

10-11

10-8

STEP 4

Fill in any needed fin detail with plastic wood *(figure 10-12)*. If a scale on the body is too loose, cut it off and fill in with plastic wood. It can be glued down with epoxy, but cutting it off is safer.

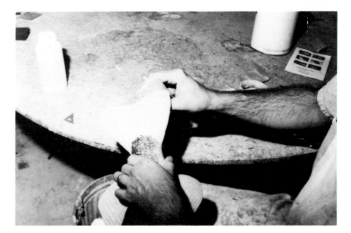

10-14

10-12

STEP 5

Paint all dry fins with primer surfacer thinned with about half as much lacquer thinner *(figure 10-13)*. This shows up any irregularities and pin holes. When the paint drys, sand fins with #150 sandpaper — only on rough edges to knock off any burrs of primer *(figure 10-14)*. Make any further fin repairs that become visible, using plastic wood and go back over the fins again with primer surfacer. Finally, sand with #220 sandpaper.

10-13

STEP 6

Seal the entire fish (even gills) by brushing on fresh, clear shellac mixed with an equal amount of solox. The fish should dry in about two hours.

PAINTING TIPS

There are some general points I would like to make in additional to earlier comments. Some are "common sense" but are important enough to be included as reminders.

1. Acrylic lacquer paint is compatible with most types of air brushes. Paint pigments vary greatly, and it is very important to add the correct amount of lacquer thinner. First, be sure the paint store thoroughly mixes the pigment — about five minutes on the shaker machine should be enough. Then when you thin it to use in the air brush, a general guide would be to put a quart of pigment into a gallon milk jug and add lacquer thinner to the base of the handle, making about three quarts of spraying consistency paint. Shake the milk jug vigorously until contents are well mixed, you can't mix the paint too much.

2. Paints work best at 72°F. When the weather is cold, more thinner is necessary. Store paints on a high shelf in the winter, since heat rises in a room.

3. If a color changes or darkens during painting, the pigment has probably settled to the bottom. It should also be noted that fluorescent lights make colors appear lighter.

4. When using larger paint spray cans (such as Paache BU Series), some pigment will remain in the tube. Be sure to spray it all out when you are finished with that color. Paint bottle tubes can be cleaned with pipe cleaners dipped in lacquer thinner.

5. Overspray spots are especially common when painting around the fins. For small paint spills, blot fin with a rag soaked with lacquer thinner. If it cannot be corrected, go back to the white and begin again (see color sequence for each species).

6. Paint residue can be a problem. It can sometimes be taken care of by changing storage jugs or filtering the paint. Be sure that paint you buy is taken from newly opened cans at the store.

7. With some things if a little is good, a lot is better. This is never true in fish painting. Too much paint kills the effects of depth and reflection.

8. Holding the air brush perpendicular to the fish can make a color look very different than painting at an angle from the tail toward the mouth. Angling from back also makes scales show up more. This is especially helpful in doing the red-orange scales of red snapper.

9. Never start to paint before a fish is completely and thoroughly dry from the preparation stage.

REPAINTING OLD FISH

Repainting a reproduction fish is usually easier than repainting skin mounts, you simply wash the fish in lacquer thinner. Skin mounts can sometimes be cleaned this way, but it can be a mess if some paint gets under the scales.

The best way to repaint skin mounts is to first test the old paint with a wire brush; if the mount seems solid, go over it with the brush. When you finish, blow all the dust off with air and paint on a thick coat of shellac. Let this coat dry completely, then apply a second coat of shellac. Let the fish dry overnight. After shellacking and drying again the next day, the skin mount should be ready to repaint.

Begin by covering the entire fish with white, passing over it several times to blot out any old color. Then apply other colors using the methods demonstrated in this book, when finished gloss as usual.

If the old mount has small cracks, fill them in with plastic wood then cover with gray primer before painting. If the cracks are bad, epoxy may be needed to fill them. Go over the fish with sandpaper and fill any pits with pin hole filler. Place lacquer thinner over the pin hole filler; cover with gray primer and the skin mount is ready to repaint.

PAINT COLORS

Listed below are the basic colors used at my studio. They obtain variety and shading as they are blended together in layers on the fish. The bass green and yellow-green are not standard paint store colors. They can be obtained from my studio, or you can mix them according to your own color preference.

1. WHITE — This goes under the belly of most fish. It is the first pigment used on freshwater fish. Use high strength white, and be sure it is dry before adding the next coat of paint — the pearl. If the pearl is added too soon, it will look molted on the fish.

2. PEARL — Pearl reflects through the remaining colors, giving the fish a lifelike appearance. When the humidity is high, the pearl will look milky when it is applied but it looks normal after it dries on the fish. Paint on enough to give the fish a slightly wet look. Several light coats are better than one heavy one. Cover everything but the mouth of the fish with pearl.
   NOTE: There is a method whereby pearl paste is mixed with lacquer gloss (called pearl essence) and painted over the colors for a sheen effect. I would recommend that you do not use this procedure because it changes the colors of the basic coats of paint.

3. SILVER (aluminum) — This is used on larger fish and on saltwater fish. Pick a silver that does not look too much like aluminum and is not too coarse or too fine (or it will lose the silvery glow). Silver is a "reading coat" and will show defects under it.

4. BASS GREEN — This can be made up using standard green, black and sienna. Use the "milk jug" mixing method, adding more lacquer thinner in the air brush bottle as needed. Bass green is our most versatile color and is the back color for bass, crappie, bream, pike, muskie, and speckled trout (thinned down). It must be sprayed on evenly to avoid light and dark areas. If you get too much on a bass, try making it darker with a mist of brown or black.

5. YELLOW-GREEN — If you use a standard yellow-green, be carefup that it does not kill the pearl. Most pigments of this color on the market are too opaque and flat. My own mixture contains yellow, green and gold, thinned twice as much as bass green (approximately 4 quarts of thinner to 1 quart pigment). Yellow-green must be used sparingly to keep the pearl effect. However, if this color is applied too thinly, you loose depth which takes away from the lifelike effect that should be achieved. Being an intangible thing, this is hard to describe but with practice you will begin to see how the thickness of one color affects the color beneath it and you will be able to apply this skill to each fish to give it an individual look. Try setting the air brush to a fine mist and go around the fish

twice. Yellow-green is usually used on fins to give them a lifelike appearance. To avoid having the overspray fall onto the fish, hold the air gun so that it angles away from the body.

6. TIE-IN GREEN — This color ties the bass green to the yellow-green. It is a standard tinting green and is used along the lateral line of the fish where the bass green meets the yellow-green.

7. ORCHID TINT — This is thinned and used lightly on speckled trout, rainbow, sailfish, marlin, bonita, and mackerel. It locks blues into deep blues and gives it a reddish tone.

8. BROWN — Best for spots and shading any fish that is predominantly yellow-green like the smallmouth bass.

9. BLACK — Mix a quart of heavy strength black with lacquer thinner in the gallon milk jug. Fins edged with black show up better. Scales show up better with a final mist of black angled toward the head. Otherwise, black should be sprayed on perpendicular to the fish. Black is usually the trim color for fish with bass green backs.

10. RED — Scarlet (or gill red) is mixed in our shop and is a good shade to use on gills. Mix a quart with lacquer thinner in a gallon jug. It should be thinned again with an equal amount of lacquer thinner to paint the sides of rainbow trout.

11. GLOSS — Use a rather fast drying gloss but one that will stay wet until the fish is completely covered. Gloss from back to front quickly and smoothly with the air brush. A large air gun is necessary to apply gloss, the air gun openings need to be cleaned with a toothpick (nothing metal) every 15-20 fish. Gloss is the most critical paint of all when painting fish. If it is applied too thickly it will run — too thinly and the fish will look flat and the quality of the pearl will be lost. Always check to make sure there is enough gloss to do the job without stopping. Let the gloss dry on the fish 30-45 minutes somewhere away from the painting area. The lacquer we use is not an automotive lacquer. It has been especially formulated to our specifications for speed of drying and enhancement of the underlying colors.

PAINTING EQUIPMENT

I cannot overstress the importance of investing in the best equipment. Success in this business depends on speed and quality of workmanship. The following is a suggested list of major equipment:

1. SAFETY PRECAUTIONS — Take note that I have put this first on the list of necessary equipment. Most paints

are made of earth pigments or oxides and precautionary measures must be taken when using them. Heavy metal content in the body can become dangerously high before it is detected. Use a double-sided activated carbon mask with a filter on the front (such as lambs wool) to catch particles (figure 10-15). An exhaust fan is not enough to protect you; always wear the mask when painting. Have a sheet metal hood made and hang curtains from it to make a painting booth (figure 10-16). The fan in my booth pulls fumes straight up; plus there are two fans in the window opposite from where I stand to pull them away from me. These may seem like extreme measures, but do take time to use them — for your health's sake.

10-15

10-16

2. AIR COMPRESSOR — (figure 10-17) Air brushes are connected by hose to a compressor, using about 30-35 pounds of pressure for paint and 40 pounds for the thicker gloss. Use quick-snap-release hoses and compatible paint cans and bottles. The compressor contains a piston which must be oiled. Though there is an oil outlet, oil can sometimes leak into the paint system and prevent paint from adhering to the fish. A good moisture trap has two gauges on it — one on the line

into the tank and one on the line coming out. As the outside temperature fluctuates, moisture can collect in the hose. It is a good idea to blow out the lines before beginning to paint. I even do it one or more times quickly during painting to clear any possible debris and to keep the paint moving smoothly.

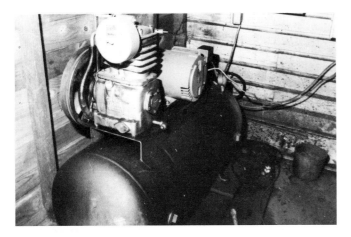

10-17

3. AIR BRUSHES — In learning to use the air brush, there is no substitute for practicing over and over on a piece of white cardboard, following the instructions that come with the air brush (figure 10-18). Listen to the sound of the spray. Learn how close to hold the gun — too close can blotch colors, and too far causes overspray, especially on small areas like fins. When changing from one color of paint to another, always spray some paint to the side to clear the brush of the first color before touching the fish. It saves time to keep air brush bottles or cans filled with paint and ready to use. There is no need to clean them out every time they are used.

For general use, there are various types and brands of good air brushes. Decide which type to use according to your needs. Many people recommend brushes

that must be manipulated with both hands but which are slower to use. Time is an important factor, when dealing with more than half a dozen fish a week. The PAACHE VL series is good for painting up to 12 or 15 fish a day. For more than that, it would be necessary to go to a larger size gun like the BU series, which takes a pint size can of paint (figure 10-19).

a. The VL is operated with one hand, and small bottles hold the paint. On top of the brush is a button operated by the forefinger that controls both the air and paint flow. Press down to release the air, and pull back to release the paint. The farther back the button is pulled, the more paint comes out. For applications needing a steady, even stream (such as stripes or even spots), adjust the roller wheel on the front (figure 10-20).

To get more volume of paint than is possible by pulling back the top button, unscrew the rear friction ring a half turn and back off on the needle until the tip is barely visible. Tighten the ring again. This saves time when using the pearl or bass green on a large number of fish. It is also possible to apply the thick gloss using this method, although it is not advisable.

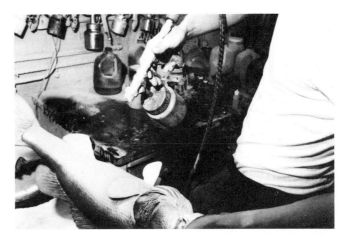

10-19

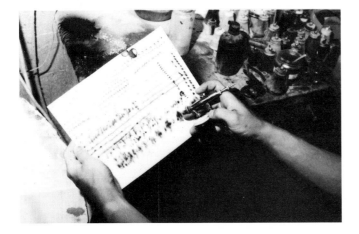

10-18

10-20

Try to keep from sloshing paint from the bottle into the air hole *(figure 10-21).* Paint with smooth, sweeping strokes. It is good to use a silicone base lubricant on the operating button periodically.

b. The BU series, or larger volume gun, is definitely better when applying gloss. There is one trigger handle that lets air and paint flow through at the same time *(figure 10-22).* Begin releasing paint just before one end of the fish, and keep it flowing past the other end. This kind of sweeping motion eliminates paint buildup and areas left unpainted.

The nozzle should be cleaned often so that the gloss will atomize properly. In addition, go around the threads often with petroleum jelly.

The paint cans come with rubber gaskets which can swell and make the lids stick. Replace these gaskets with fiber ones. The thin gasket material available at automotive parts stores can be cut to fit.

10-22

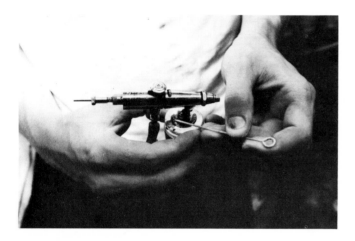

10-21

PAINTING THE LARGEMOUTH BASS (Micropterus Salmoides)

The largemouth bass is probably the most highly regarded freshwater gamefish in America, with a range covering almost the entire U.S. It is known in many parts of the country by different common names such as green trout or black bass.

Many people confuse the largemouth bass with the small mouth bass, simply by associating the size of the mouth with some criteria. The following illustrations will help you recognize the difference. The average weight for the largemouth bass is 4-10 pounds, with some weighing over 20 pounds.

1. Spray the belly white.

2. Pearl the entire outside of the fish.

3. Spray bass green along the entire upper body and upper fins. holding the fish by the tail, paint the cheek, the top of the gill, across the head, and down the other side, rolling the fish — not the air brush. Paint the back and tail. Keep the color the same density. It helps to set the wheel on the VL in a stationary position when painting six or more bass at the same time.

4. Yellow-green goes below the mid-line of the body, leaving the belly white. Then go back and touch the lower jaw, lower fins, and side fins. A thin coat of yellow-green lets the pearl show through, giving the fish depth.

5. Tie-in green goes between bass green and yellow-green, so that all three colors blend together. Start on the back side; come lightly across the cheek and then down the other side. Spray lightly along the edges of the upper fins.

6. Adjust the air brush for painting smaller areas. Using black now put the row of diamond shapes down the middle of the sides, moving your hand in what I call a "sewing machine" pattern. The paint hits the fish in the middle of each swing, making the spots uneven and not round — more natural than the round spots made by simply pressing the spray button on and off. The faster this can be done, the more natural the fish looks.

7. Make a generally diamond shaped pattern above the lateral scale line using black. It should be indistinct and look molted.

8. Paint the lips black.

9. Make thick rows of dots radiating from the eye and circle the eye with black.

10. Finish the back of the fish with the molted diamond pattern that most resembles the fish you are painting. Remember, it is not important to match your specimen dot for dot, this would be impossible. Paint in the general methods described, emphasizing the individual qualities that your fish has.

11. Make three or four rows of spots below the mid-line still using black. Make them with the air brush very close to the fish at a slight upward angle so that they are not exactly round. Turn the fish up — not the brush. Pick out a scale line and follow this down the body each time.

12. Slightly spray the fins at an angle from the back, just enough to bring out the ridges in them. Trim the edges at an angle away from the fish to avoid overspray onto the body. Angle more onto the tail and add a few thin light lines to it and to the lower fins.

13. Mist the upper body with black, apply several times if the fish should be darker.

14. Apply red to cover all gills.

15. Re-spray inside the mouth with white.

16. Gloss the entire fish with wide sweeps of the air brush.

The smallmouth bass is probably one of the hardest fighters that swims.

The rainbow trout is one of our most colorful freshwater species.

The brown trout is found in the upper and western U.S.

The brook trout is excellent game for fly fishing.

The bluegill has a beautiful coloring which changes at different times of the year and in different water conditions.

Note the subtle color variations in this amberjack.

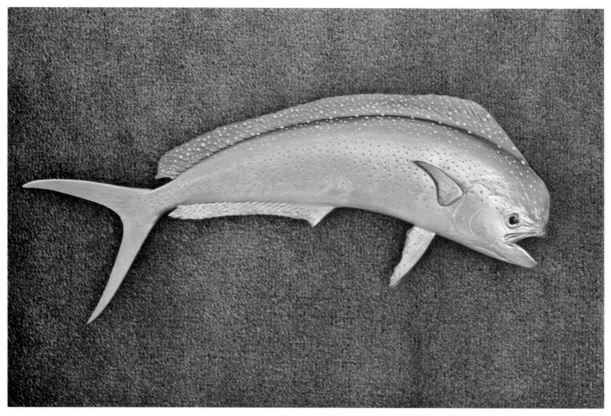

The dolphin has beautiful colors that literally light up when the fish is excited.

The jack crevalle is a saltwater fighter found throughout the world.

Hammerhead sharks grow to ten feet and longer.

The black tip shark is one of the most common sharks.

The king mackerel is a very popular fish for trolling boats and is excellent seafood.

The Atlantic sailfish is a highly prized trophy of the saltwater sportsman.

MOUNTING TIPS

REPAIRING TROUT HEADS

A common problem often encountered in mounting trout is shrinkage in the head after drying. I have found a couple of good ways to fix this that are both simple and inexpensive.

One way is to use plastic wood on the sunken area. Apply it with a spatula, then dip the spatula in lacquer thinner and smooth it out *(figure 11-1)*. When you have it

the way you want it, let it dry, then brush primer surface over the area and sand smooth.

The epoxy method also works well. There are many different types of epoxies that can be used. We often use plumbers putty *(figure 11-2)*. and a product called Plyacre also does a good job.

Mix the resin and hardener in equal amounts and make sure it is blended well. Apply where necessary on the fish's head, in all dented and hollow spots *(figure 11-3)*. Smooth and sculpture it with your fingers. Dipping your

11-1

11-2

fingers in water makes this easier. Work it until a smooth head appears *(figure 11-4).*

Sanding is unnecessary if the job is done well, however, if there is a little irregularity, a light sanding may be in order.

11-3

11-4

CLEANING ARTIFICIAL FISH EYES

(New way to mask fish eyes before painting that will save you time and money)

For years the taxidermist has been plagued with the problem of scraping the surplus paint off fish eyes after the mount has been painted. I have tried many methods such as smearing vaseline, latex rubber, wax, clay, among other things over the eye. Many times the trouble of getting these things off was worse than simply painting over the glass itself and then taking a scalpel and slowing removing the paint.

While at Piedmont Tech for their annual mini-course on taxidermy, I asked the audience if they had any ideas on how to do this in a fast way. I got all kinds of answers. In my commercial booth, a fellow named Doug Tron, from Maryville came up to me and explained a method that he had had luck with. It involved using a rubber "o" ring with masking tape over one end and sticky double-sided tape in the middle. This sounded like a good idea to me and when I came home, I gave it a try. I worked and worked with it but could not get the nice clean finish that I thought was possible. For one thing, I was putting my eyes in with papier-mache and the edges that came up to the glass eye, were not smooth enough to give a clean break when the ring was removed.

I discarded this idea for the time being and continued as I had been doing. I talked with some folks who were using several types of epoxy for sculpturing the sunken heads of trout and they were putting their fish eyes in with "Plyacre" — which we mentioned in the repairing of trout heads. A light bulb immediately went on in my head. If the eye were placed in the fish with this medium, and slicked down by dipping the fingers into water and working it smooth, I knew that it would enable me to use the "o" ring method.

As I experimented with the method, it became apparent that the plyacre must be smoothed up to the very edge of the eye, right to the place where it makes its sharp turn downward. The contour of the material must be exactly right, and perfectly round, the same as the eye — no sloppy work.

I worked out my first batch of fish and was elated, but I saw that I still had some small problems to overcome. I had used rings that were just slightly too large for the eye, and a light ring of plyacre showed up. I realized that the airbrush will deflect the paint when it hits the edge of the ring and this will cause the ring to actually mask a larger circle than it covers. I remedied this by using a ring slightly smaller than the eye, and the next batch were perfect.

The neat part of this method is that when the spray hits the rubber ring, there is a clean break with the other paint surfaces and when the paint is dry, you can peel up the ring from one side without peeling any of the paint up around the eye. The "o" rings can be bought at most hardware stores and you can use the same ones over and over again.

Take as many #212 "o" rings as you think you will need, line them up in a row and lay a strip of masking tape down on top of these. Press it down hard to make the "o" rings stick to it, then turn the tape over so that the rings are facing upward. The #212 "o" ring is the right size for a 20 mm eye.

Get some double-sided carpet tape and cut some squares, small enough to fit down into the "o" ring, out of a piece *(figure 11-5)*. Press this tape into place and cut the rings apart, trimming away the excess tape around the edges *(figure 11-6)*.

Mark these for identification purposes with a felt tip pen and store them in a sealable container to keep dust off them.

After the eye is inserted in the fish and the mount is ready to paint, simply stick one of these "o" rings on the eye, making sure you center it properly and press it firmly into place *(figure 11-7)*.

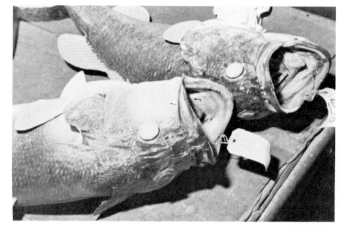

11-7

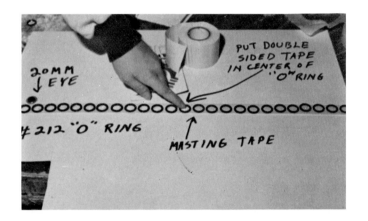

11-5

A QUICK METHOD OF FISH FIN BACKING

The splits and irregularities on the fins of fish, especially the tail are a natural occurrence and is worse on some fish than others. To fix this, stick a piece of two inch masking tape onto the back of the fin, pressing it hard to make it stick firmly *(figure 11-8)*.

Trim this tape to the general contour of the fin, cutting off the tip of the fin if necessary to make it shape up good *(figure 11-9)*.

Apply some white glue, Elmers glue works well, to the top of the fin and spread it with a small paint brush to seal all

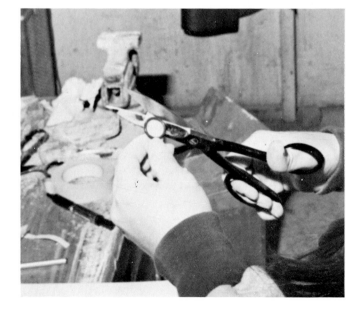

11-6

11-8

of the cracks and exposed tape *(figure 11-10)*. If necessary cover the entire fin with the glue. Smearing the glue with your finger also works well. I use Elmers glue because it has some properties that will seal in any excess oil deposits that sometimes have a tendency to leak out at the base of the tail.

PUTTING FISH ON PANEL

To put the fish on a panel, begin by drilling two holes into the back of the fish where the wooden block is *(figure 11-11)*. Next lay the fish at the desired angle on the panel and some sawdust should fall out of the holes onto the panel *(figure 11-12)*. Mark these spots and drill these holes into the panel.

Attach the fish with screws, putting the back screw in first. Line up the front holes, then insert this screw. If it doesn't line up properly, drill another hole.

11-9

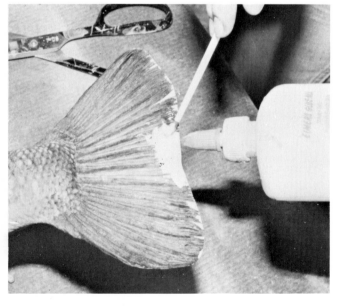

11-10

11-11

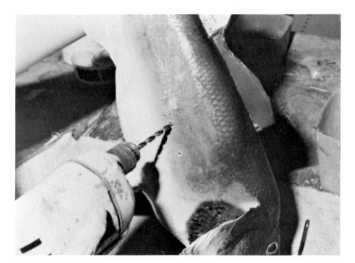

11-12

TAXIDERMY SUPPLY SOURCES

Bill Allen
Route 940
White Haven, Pennsylvania

L. M. Rathbone
Austin Taxidermist
Star Route A Box 769E
Austin, Texas 78746

Reel Trophy
P. O. Box 19085
Portland, Oregon 97219

Jonas Brothers
Taxidermist Supplies
Denver, Colorado 80203

J. W. Elwood and Co.
Omaha, Nebraska 68102

G. Schoepfer
134 West 32nd Street
New York, New York 10001

Clearfield Taxidermy
603 Hannah Street
Clearfield, Pennsylvania 16830

McKenzie Supply Co.
P. O. Box 480
Granite Quarry, North Carolina

Wilderness Supply Co.
5118 Tulane Street
Jackson, Mississippi 39209

Touchstone Taxidermy Supply
Route 1, Box 5294
Bossier City, Louisiana 71111

Mackrell Taxidermy, Inc.
Con Cordville, Pennsylvania 19331

Dan Chase
Route 2, Box 317A
Baker, Louisiana 70714

North Star Freeze Dry
Box 439
Pegout, Minnesota 56472

Archie Phillips
200 52nd Street
Fairfield, Alabama 35064
(Fish Blanks)

Knopp Brothers
Taxidermy Studios
N. 6715 Division Street
Spokane, Washington 99208

Arco Taxidermy Supplies
Box 693
Tarpon Springs, Florida 33589

Nippon Panel Co.
South Williamsport, Pennsylvania 17707
(Plaques and shields only)

Chandler's Mounting Panels
206 Eisenhower Street
Jackson, Mississippi 39209
(Plaques, shields and forms)

Continental Felt Company
22 West 15th Street
New York, New York 10011
(Felt only)

E. L. Heacock Company
117 Bleecker Street
Gloversville, New York 12078
(Products made from tanned skins you supply)

Burnham Brothers
P. O. Box 100
Marble Falls, Texas 78654
(Knives and sharpening devices)

Van Dyke
Woonsocket, South Dakota 57385

Meyer Fish Mix
4783 N. Bend Road
Cincinnati, Ohio 45211

Commonwealth Felt Company
160 Fifth Avenue
New York, New York 10016
(Felt only)

TAXIDERMY CORRESPONDENCE COURSES

Northwestern School of Taxidermy
P. O. Box 3507
Omaha, Nebraska 68103

Taxidermy Success Training
Route 1 Box 5294
Bossier City, Louisiana 71111

American Wildlife Studios
P. O. Box 16030
Baton Rouge, Louisiana 70803

Taxidermy Supply Company
P. O. Box 5815-T
Bossier City, Louisiana 71010

Devereaux Taxidermy School
P. O. Box 373
Point Lookout, Missouri

Missouri School of Taxidermy
Lake Road, Poplar Bluff, Mo. 63901

SCHOOLS

Piedmont Tech
Roxoboro, N.C. 27573

American Institute of Taxidermy
3918-3232 McCormick
Janesville, WI 53545

Freeze Dry School
Vic Brontas
Box 212
Nisswa, Minn. 56468

TAXIDERMY MAGAZINES

Modern Taxidermist
Greenfield Center, New York 12833

Taxidermy Review
675 Columbine Street
Denver, Colorado 80206

American Taxidermist
P. O. Box 11186
Albuquerque, New Mexico 87112

Touch Stone Taxidermy Art
Route 1, Box 5294
Bossier City, La. 71111

Taxidermy Today
3232 McCormick Dr.
Janesville, WI 53545